L. J. Kutten, an attorney and computer hobbyist, specializes in computer and high-technology law. He has written a number of articles dealing with such subjects as computer copyrights, employment contracts, and antitrust law. He is a member of the Illinois and Missouri Bars, and he lives in St. Louis, Missouri.

L. J. KUTTEN

COMPUTER BUYER'S PROTECTION GUIDE

HOW TO PROTECT YOUR RIGHTS IN THE MICROCOMPUTER MARKETPLACE

Prentice-Hall, Inc. / Englewood Cliffs, N.J. 07632

Library of Congress Cataloging in Publication Data

Kutten, L. J.
  Computer buyer's protection guide.

  "A Spectrum Book."
  Includes index.
  1. Computers—Specifications—United States.
  2. Computers—Purchasing. 3. Commercial law—United
States. I. Title.
  KF915.Z93C654 1984   343.73′07800164   83-21218
  ISBN 0–13–164195–6   347.307800164
  ISBN 0–13–164187–5 (pbk.)

This publication is designed to provide accurate and authoritative information in regard to the subject matter covered. It is sold with the understanding that the publisher is not engaged in rendering legal, accounting, or other professional service. If legal advice or other expert assistance is required, the services of a competent professional person should be sought.

—*From a Declaration of Principles jointly adopted by a Committee of the American Bar Association and a Committee of Publishers and Associations.*

This book is available at a special discount when ordered
in bulk quantities. Contact Prentice-Hall, Inc., General
Publishing Division, Special Sales, Englewood Cliffs, N. J. 07632.

ISBN 0-13-164195-6

0-13-164187-5 {PBK.}

Prentice-Hall International, Inc., *London*
Prentice-Hall of Australia Pty. Limited, *Sydney*
Prentice-Hall of Canada Inc., *Toronto*
Prentice-Hall of India Private Limited, *New Delhi*
Prentice-Hall of Japan, Inc., *Tokyo*
Prentice-Hall of Southeast Asia Pte. Ltd., *Singapore*
Whitehall Books Limited, *Wellington, New Zealand*
Editora Prentice-Hall do Brasil Ltda., *Rio de Janeiro*

Dedicated To:

David Vernon, Professor of Law, who first taught me how to think like a lawyer; David Welsh, whose word processing program, Lazy Writer, took the drudgery out of writing; and most important, to my wife Linda, without whose encouragement (and patience) this book never would have been completed.

Contents

1

So You Want To Buy a Computer

2

General Hardware and Software Considerations

3
The Law of Sales

4

Where Will You Buy From?
Locally vs. Mail Order

5

How to Pay

6

The Law of Warranties

7

Acceptance and Rejection of Goods

8

How to Complain Effectively

9

Miscellaneous Hints and Suggestions

Index

Preface

Between 1976 and 1982, the personal computer marketplace grew from nothing to over $6 billion in worldwide sales. Market analysts predict that 1986 sales will exceed $20 billion. As a result, the great microcomputer rip-offs have begun. No longer are microcomputers bought only by computer hackers or system analysts; they are bought by everyday people who see them as the panacea for their problems. A parent buys one thinking it will be his child's key to success in school; a business executive gets one thinking it will increase productivity. This list could go on and on. God knows how many $3000 computers are bought so a child can play PAC-MAN at home.

Book stores are being flooded with computer books. The general thrust of these books is to tell you what computer to buy or how to program. This book does neither. I do not care what computer you buy, whether it be an APPLE, an IBM PC, a TRS-80, or whatever. What I do care about is your not getting defrauded.

The impetus to write this book sprang from my participation in COMPUSERVE's MNET80 special interest group. MNET80 is a group of TRS-80 enthusiasts who use their microcomputers to communicate electronically. The information passed back and forth ranges from what equipment to avoid to the weather in Atlanta.

When I first joined MNET80, I was shocked by the number of people who have had trouble while buying microcomputer hardware and software. A typical complaint message is as follows:

I recently ordered some equipment from a retailer. I paid a $1000 deposit by money order and was supposed to get three (3) different pieces. A month later, he called me and said he had "accidentally" sold one of the three pieces. He then asked me to take a different piece, which he said was in excellent condition, for an additional $1500. I agreed. After a long wait, the $1500 piece arrived but not the other two. After calling many times, and having four months go by, I bought a second machine from someone else for $1800. He still has my original $1000, and I had to spend $1000 fixing up the second machine. It was not in excellent condition. What can I do?

This story is not unique. It seemed as if everyone I talked with had trouble at one time or another in getting satisfaction with the goods he had purchased: It was usually either his own fault, lack of communication between himself and the vendor, misleading advertisements, and sometimes fraud.

Although the consumer did not know it, the law was on his side. Many times I left messages suggesting practical solutions or explained the general law behind the problem. After a while, I realized I was repeating myself. Thus, this book was born.

This book is the first to deal exclusively with the law and microcomputers. If you buy an automobile or a television set and have a problem, there are books and consumer groups available to help resolve the problem. These resources do not exist for buyers of microcomputers. The microcomputer industry has grown so fast that consumer support groups have not had time to catch up. Although this book alone will not fill this missing gap, by using the information in it, you will become a knowledgeable microcomputer consumer.

This book will assist you in buying a microcomputer. It assumes you have no prior experience in buying a microcomputer, that you have no knowledgeable friends to advise you, and that you do not know about the practical problems of buying a microcomputer and its peripheral equipment.

I have tried to pull together most of the questions and legal points to consider before, during, and after making any microcomputer-oriented purchase. These tips, comments, and suggestions have been applied time and again by me and by other computer hobbyists. They come out of my experiences as an attorney and computer hobbyist for the past six years. They will help you avoid the many pitfalls that have befallen me, my clients, and others.

Nine areas will be covered:

1. A survey of some points to consider before buying a computer.
2. Some general considerations regarding hardware and software.
3. A general introduction to the law concerning the buying and selling of goods.
4. Buying from a mail order company versus a local store.

5. The pitfalls and protection of paying by cash, credit, check, and money order.
6. What warranties really cover.
7. How to reject and revoke a prior acceptance of a product.
8. How to complain effectively if a product does not work.
9. Miscellaneous hints, tricks of the trade, and suggestions.

I have tried to keep my discussion of the law and various statutes simple. Most of the general principles discussed are as valid in Maine as in Hawaii. These hints, points, and suggestions can apply to most cases.

Throughout this book there are references to various federal and state statutes and court cases. The citations given are standardized. Any law library, regardless of where it is located (if you do not know of one nearby, call the local courthouse) will show you the same case if you ask to see 343 F.2d 456 or 34 United States Code §115 (more commonly cited as 34 U.S.C. §115).

The Uniform Commercial Code references are to the 1972 model version as currently proposed by the National Conference of Commissioners on Uniform State Laws.

Many of the microcomputer examples in this book mention Radio Shack's TRS-80 MODEL I and MODEL III microcomputers. These examples should neither be considered a disparagement nor an endorsement of Radio Shack or its computers. They were used because I am most familiar with them. I bought one of the first Radio Shack TRS-80 MODEL Is sold in St. Louis. Although I have experience with a wide variety of microcomputers, I continue to use the TRS-80 MODEL III primarily.

The advice in this book is broad, and I have attempted to present a "worst case" scenario (it happens more times than you think). Many of the comments and suggestions require that you do some work. The decision to do this work should be pragmatic. For example, there is no need to protect a $10 purchase with the same safeguards as $1000 purchase. Finally, nothing in this book should be construed as giving legal advice in any particular situation. The facts in a particular case may call for an entirely different course of action.

L. J. KUTTEN, Attorney at Law
St. Louis, Missouri

Acknowledgments

I wish to acknowledge the generous help of Peggy McDermott, Washington University Law School Reference Librarian, in finding the applicable statutes, government reports, and court cases mentioned throughout this book. I owe another large debt to Bob Snapp of Snappware, Inc., who provided information on the technical and operational methods of personal computers and the microcomputer industry.

Trademark Acknowledgments

ACE-1000 is a registered trademark of Franklin Computer Corp.
ALTOS is a registered trademark of Altos Computers Systems.
APPLE, APPLE II/e, APPLE III, and LISA are registered trademarks of
      Apple Computer Inc.
ATARI is a registered trademark of Atari, Inc.
ATTACHE COMPTER is a registered trademark of Otrona Corp.
BASF is a registered trademark of BASF Systems Corp.
COMMODORE 64 and VIC-20 are registered trademarks of Commodore
      Computer Systems, Inc.
COMPUSERVE is a registered trademark of CompuServe, Inc.
DOSPLUS is a registered trademark of Micro-Management Systems,
      Inc.
DOW JONES NEWS/RETRIEVAL is a registered trademark of Dow Jones
      & Co.
DYSAN is a registered trademark of the Dysan Corp.

ELECTRIC WEBSTER is a registered trademark of Cornucopia Software.

IBM PC is a registered trademark of International Business Machines Corp.

KAYPRO 10 is a registered trademark of Kay Computers.

LAZY WRITER program is a registered trademark of Alpha Bit Communications, Inc.

LEXIS is a registered trademark of Mead Data Corp.

LEXITRON is a registered trademark of Raytheon Corp.

LDOS is a registered trademark of Logical Systems, Inc.

NEWDOS is a registered trademark of Apparat, Inc.

QUME is a registered trademark of Qume Corporation.

RADIO SHACK, TRS-80, and SUPERSCRIPSIT is a registered trademark of Tandy Corp.

RAINBOW 100 is a registered trademark of Digital Equipment Corp.

SINCLAIR is a registered trademark of Sinclair Research, Inc.

SOOPERSPOOLER is a registered trademark of Compulink Corp.

TEXAS INSTRUMENTS is a registered trademark of Texas Instruments.

THE SOURCE is a registered trademark of Source Telecomputing Corp.

VERBATIM is a registered trademark of Verbatim Corp.

VISICALC is a registered trademark of Personal Software, Inc.

XEROX and DIABLO is a registered trademark of Xerox Corp.

WORDSTAR is a registered trademark of MicroPro, Inc.

1

So You Want
to Buy a Computer

So you want to buy a computer. This is fine and dandy. There is nothing wrong with your wanting a computer, provided you answer "Yes" to the following question: "Do I really need a computer?" For most people the answer is "No."

Microcomputer manufacturers have spent millions upon millions of dollars trying to convince the American public to buy their products. The advertisements try to convince you that you *need* a computer. A computer is supposedly a panacea to all our problems—by using a computer you will reach the utopia of a better job, more money, or smarter children. *Nothing is further from the truth!*

People gladly spend $3000 on a computer to play chess, balance a checkbook, keep a Christmas mailing list, or to play video arcade games. The average consumer does not do a cost/benefit analysis. Were the cost of expenditures compared to the benefits received, the consumer would quickly realize that for 99% of the things he or she wants done, there is a cheaper, noncomputerized way of doing it.

How the Personal Computer Sales Industry Works

The average microcomputer buyer usually walks into a computer store and tells a "computer consultant" (more commonly known as a sales clerk) that he thinks he wants a computer. The sales clerk demonstrates one or two systems and gives him some literature. The buyer returns three or four times before buying. If there are any children in the family, he usually buys the same kind of computer his child uses in school.

1

You and the vendor approach buying a computer from different perspectives. You feel you are buying a solution to a problem. You expect the equipment to be delivered one day and working the next. You do not expect a long period between installation and actual productive use. You walk into the situation like a steer heading for the slaughterhouse.

The vendor, represented by a commissioned salesperson, has a different goal. He is perfectly willing to let you keep your unrealistic expectations about what the computer will do. The vendor feels he is only selling specified hardware or software; he does not nor will he guarantee a solution to a specific problem. He knows that every user will experience difficulties in the beginning.

The salesperson wants to close the sale and get his commission; he makes the situation as pleasant and quick as possible. The salesperson (if he is any good) knows how to get the buyer hooked on the line and reeled in.

No first-time buyer ever realizes the long-term consequences of his actions: Hardware needs to be maintained and fixed; complex software will have "bugs" and flaws that will need to be fixed; and these repairs will have to be made by the vendor.

> *Example 1-1:* During the past five years either I or friends of mine have had the following experiences. (Each software program was released by a major distributor in each case.)
>
> 1. A communications package (i.e., a program that would allow a microcomputer to speak to another computer such as COMPUSERVE or The SOURCE) could not speak to the DOW JONES NEWS/RETRIEVAL computer.
>
> 2. A stock portfolio program could not accept American Airlines' preferred quarterly stock divided, $0.28 7/8 ($0.28875); it could go only three decimal places.
>
> 3. A checkbook program would not accept $29.32 as a valid numerical entry.
>
> 4. A word processing program was advertised as allowing text files of unlimited size. After 10 pages, it got internally lost and destroyed the text files.
>
> 5. The Apple Computer Company replaced all Apple IIIs with a serial number below 14,000 because of serious hardware problems.

A businessperson is in a worse position than a consumer. First, she has a business to run; she cannot take time from her busy schedule to investigate the matter. She usually assigns one of her employees to research the problem. This person does not necessarily understand or even know of all the details of her employer's business operations. Second, the businessperson needs the system immediately. She has a pressing problem that needed to be solved yesterday.

The businessperson fails to ask a number of important questions:

1. Where can I see the identical (or as close as possible) system (both hardware and software) installed?
2. How do I get my existing data into the system, and how much will it cost?
3. Can the system generate forms (e.g., invoices, statements) similar to my present forms? If so, show me a current user who is generating similar forms.
4. How long a wait is there usually between installation and 100% operational use?
5. What specific warranties are offered on the software?
6. What happens if the system fails and destroys my diskette (especially important when using protected software)?
7. What is the documented down time between the time the system fails and when it can be repaired?
8. When does the warranty period begin? Does it start when the goods are delivered or when the system becomes operational?

The business buyer faces one additional danger that the average consumer does not: the account executive. There are many office supply companies selling computers and word processors. They have account executives (sales people) who will come to the potential buyer's business office instead of the buyer's going to the showroom. Does the buyer want to see a unit in operation? No problem. The account executive will bring one out for a demonstration. Does the businessperson want to try it for a short period? No problem, it can stay for a week or two. Do not think the account executive or her employer is being altruistic. They are cold and calculating. They do not want a businessperson to comparison shop. They know that if he did, he might not buy from them.

> *Example 1-2:* A local account executive once tried to sell me a word processing system. Part of the package was a $4500 name brand printer. The same printer was available at a local computer store for $2500. The major difference between the units was the nameplates and the name on the instruction manual.

Things to Know Before Buying a Microcomputer

There are many very important points to consider before buying a microcomputer that the vendor will not mention unless you specifically ask about them.

1. *The computer may not work properly without additional expensive wiring.* A computer is a delicate electrical device; it expects to receive a steady amount of voltage (115–125 volts AC). If for any reason the voltage fluctuates out of this range, the computer may not work; the disk drives will not turn at the right speed needed to load information; the memory chips will become unstable and lose data.

> *Example 1-3:* A particular computer may be on the same circuit as a photocopy machine. Every time the photocopy machine is used, it momentarily draws a large amount of power. The amount of power to the computer first falls, then it surges when the photocopy machine stops. This surge could cause the computer to crash.

This problem also exists in older homes and buildings. As more and more electrical devices have been added, the demands on the power being brought into these older buildings has increased. The 100 amp service prevalent 20 years ago when these buildings were built is no longer sufficient. Just think of the new electrical devices that were not commonplace then: video tape recorders, central air conditioning, microwave ovens. The electric typewriters, televisions, and stereos will work without difficulty but not the computer.

As a side point to this problem, not all computers will react the same. My TRS-80 Model I continually crashed when it was in one office, yet the TRS-80 Model III worked without a single problem in the same office, out of the same electrical plug.

2. *Employees may be reluctant to use the new computer.* Some people are afraid of the new. If they approach the computer with fear or take their hostility out against it, they can easily damage it.

3. *You and your employees may have to change your work habits.* Computers are very susceptible to dust. If someone chain smokes around a typewriter, it is no big deal. The typewriter will not crash or have problems because ashes were "accidentally" dropped into its mechanisms. If the same ashes get inside a disk drive the unit will have to be "professionally" (and expensively) cleaned. Likewise, a magnetic paper clip holder does not affect a typewriter. Put the same magnetic paper clip holder next to a diskette, and the data contained on the diskette may be destroyed.

4. *Training employees to use the computer may cause a temporary loss of productivity.* It is not easy to learn how to use a computer or software. For example, with Visicalc, it is estimated that it takes 30 hours to learn how to use 75% of the program's capability, another 15 hours to learn how to use another 20% of it, and the rest of your life to learn the remaining 5%.

Many vendors run classes to teach users how to use their systems. This is not as good as it sounds. A manufacturer of a $7,000 word processing system conducts a two-day training seminar in which a 300-page manual is reviewed. Most people take longer than that to learn how to drive an automobile.

5. *You are not told how expensive it can be to convert your data (whether it be a mailing list or accounts receivable) from one system to another.* Many times the cost of conversion exceeds the cost of the hardware and software.

6. *At no time are you warned that there is a good chance that the entire system will fail to operate properly.* According to one expert who testified in *Chatlos Systems vs. National Cash Register Corp.*, DNJ 1979, 479 F. Supp. 738, over 40% of minicomputer installations fail to operate properly. There is no reason to expect that microcomputer installations will be different.

7. *Finally, you are never warned not to dismantle or quit using your present system until there is* absolutely *no doubt that the new system is working as expected.* Because you automatically expect the system to work perfectly, you quit using your present system. It is not until months later, once you realize that something is wrong, that you must rush to reconcile your previous work.

> *Example 1-3:* A client bought a checkbook maintenance program. After five months of operation, it started rejecting certain numbers (e.g., $29.32) as valid numerical entries. A disk with the problem was shipped to the software publisher for review. The publisher claimed they had accidentally shipped the wrong version, which was still undergoing testing. They replaced it with an older version that was claimed to work. The older version could *not* read the five months of data that had been stored by the newer version.

How to Buy

There are a number of steps to follow before you buy any computer.

1. *Identify major uses.* Decide what is the primary reason that impels you to buy a computer. Do you want to play video games and teach yourself the basics of programming? Do you want to do sophisticated stock analysis and financial modeling? Do you want to run inventory and payroll programs for a small business? Once you know what you want to do with the computer, you can quickly eliminate those computers that are not designed for that primary use.

2. *First find the software and then the computer.* Advertising claims notwithstanding, no one can learn to program in BASIC or any

computer language in two hours or two weeks any more than anyone can become fluent in a foreign language in two weeks.

Most consumers buy software written by professionals (at least one *hopes* they are professionals). Those consumers are the "settlers" who need a trail boss to lead the wagon train and protect them. It is the rare consumer who becomes the self-reliant programming "cowboy."

When evaluating software for any particular computer, always examine the amount of software available for *that machine*. Look at the depth and breadth of programs available. Are there programs for word processing, spreadsheets, payroll, accounts receivable, inventory control? If there are only one or two programs per application, be wary.

Never assume that the price of software has anything to do with its utility or usefulness.

> *Example 1-4:* Some word processing programs have additional programs that support mathematical functions. The additional program can automatically add, subtract, divide, and multiply numbers in a document. On one system, this package cost $500. On another, $20.
>
> *Example 1-5:* In May, 1982, the manufacturer of JRT Pascal dropped the price from $295 to $29.95.

Warning: Many vendors claim their machine is CP/M compatible. *This is a half-truth.* CP/M is a computer operating system developed by Digital Research. Any program written in CP/M will run on a computer capable of operating CP/M. The problem is that there is no standard for storing information on a 5¼-inch diskette. The problem is similar to that faced by people who own video tape recorders. Although a Beta and VHS video tape may contain the same movie, a VHS machine cannot run a Beta tape and a Beta machine cannot run a VHS tape. Or as IBM expressed it: To get IBM's CP/M-86 to support existing CP/M-80 application programs, it will be necessary for "the data and programs files . . . [to be] converted to the diskette format used by the IBM Personal Computer."

3. *Computers are very expensive.* Do not think you are getting a full-fledged computer for $300. All you get is a stripped-down version. The options quickly raise the price. A good quality printer costs a minimum of $1000. Floppy disk drives start at $300 (serious users will want a hard drive at $1500). A modem, $300. Full-feature word processing or data-base software, $300.

It is an accepted fact in microcomputer sales that the average consumer will spend roughly as much within 18 months on additional software, accessories, and the like as he did in making the original purchase. According to market research conducted by Frost and Sullivan, the average buyer of personal computers spends $608 on initial purchases of software or programming. During the next year, he spends an additional $439 on software.

Many sellers would gladly give away the base unit if they could be guaranteed that their customers would buy all the peripherals and software from them.

4. *Survey sources of information.* Do not believe everything the sales clerk or account executive tells you. Check things for yourself. Various sources of information include trade magazines, product reviews, and users' groups.

Magazines

Before buying any microcomputer, find out from any dealer what magazines specialize in it (e.g., *PC Magazine* for the IBM PC, *80-Micro* for the TRS-80, *Nibble* for the APPLE). Go to the local library and read the past 12 months' issues. If the library does not have the magazine, order back issues from the publisher. The letters to the editors will tell you what the owners like and dislike about the computers they have bought. Reading the advertisements will show the depth and breadth of third-party support.

Product Reviews:

Do not pay too much attention to product reviews. You could spend years before finding a negative review. According to Eric Maloney, managing editor of *80-Micro*, there are eight main reasons why there are almost no negative reviews:

1. In the early days of computer magazines, those persons who wrote software also wrote for the magazines.
2. Many publishers feel that if something good cannot be said about a piece of hardware or software, do not say anything.
3. Reviewers are computer enthusiasts who tend to be enthusiastic about everything.
4. As enthusiasts, reviewers get a great charge out of anything new and interesting. As a result, they are too forgiving of the negative aspects of a new or interesting product. Because of their experience, they know how to make it work, regardless of the instructions.
5. Reviewers are into reviewing primarily to get free products and do not want to jeopardize their supply.
6. Reviewers tend to be software authors and are afraid of getting slammed themselves.
7. Many editors do not have a computer background and cannot see the potential flaws in a reviewer's perceptions.
8. Many computer editors do not have an editorial background and do not see the flaws in a reviewer's writing.

Another reason for the lack of negative reviews is the amount of advertising revenue spent by large companies. Very few editors will attack a company that spends $5,000 a month advertising in his magazine.

Warning: Before buying any expensive product, see it in actual use. Find out the name of a local user and talk with him or her. There are three reasons for doing this:

1. Even briefly using the product or talking with someone who has used it can acquaint you with many of its shortcomings.
2. If the product is new, you do not want to be a guinea pig. Let someone else have the aggravation of reporting software bugs or hardware quirks!
3. You will be assured that the product actually exists and is being shipped. Many times, computer equipment and programs are reviewed or advertised months before they become commercially available.

If you do not see the product in actual use, then what happened to the Glovatorium company can happen to you. According the Ninth Circuit Court of Appeals in *The Glovatorium, Inc.* v. *NCR Corporation*, 1982, 684 F.2d 658, the NCR Corporation sold a hardware and software package known as SPIRIT, which was supposedly capable of "route accounting":

> [O]ne of the problems experienced with the system was that it was so slow that many clients found they could accomplish the same task faster if it were done manually rather than using the SPIRIT system. . . . NCR, however developed and distributed a demonstrator model for the system to be used as a sales tool that "was specifically designed to function very, very effectively, and very fast, much more so than the actual SPIRIT programs did."

Users' Groups

Join a local users' group for the computer you have or plan to buy. If there is none, then join a general computer group. The members know all the nitty-gritty details of the computer and its local dealers—who has the best and worst service technicians; who is friendly to deal with, and who is a pain in the butt. It is the cheapest and quickest source of information. Just by asking questions, you can learn from someone else's experience with a specific piece of hardware, software, or dealer. If there are no local clubs, then join one of the national users' groups. A number of these exist for a variety of hardware and software. These groups include a national CP/M user group, a national Visicalc user group, and a national Apple computer user group.

Warning: Some local users' groups are no more than meeting places for software trading and piracy. Neither the federal government nor software publishers look kindly on this. If software piracy is conducted openly at your local meetings, you could be held both civilly and *criminally* liable. Software copying without authorization is a crime!

2

General Hardware and Software Considerations

The Major Commandment

If you follow only one rule, follow this one: *Let someone else be the guinea pig.* Never be the first one on the block with a new toy. Every new piece of major hardware or software has had design difficulties. This rule even applies to new versions of previously released hardware or software. Fixing one problem can cause another. Too many companies will gladly let you field test their hardware or software instead of incurring the expenses themselves.

Hardware

Because of the explosive growth in microcomputer sales, companies are entering the microcomputer field left and right. Currently there are over 120 different brands available. Major names include Apple, Atari, Commodore, Corvus, Cromemco, Digital Equipment, Epson, Fortune, Franklin, Hewlett-Packard, IBM, Kaypro, Nippon Electric Company, North Star, Otrona, Olivetti, Osborne, Panasonic, Radio Shack, Sharp, Sony, Texas Instruments, Timex, Victor, Wang, and Xerox. All these companies manufacture microcomputers, and that is about all they have in common. Many of the smaller companies will not be in existence five years from now.

Many well-known consumer electronics companies now sell or manufacture microcomputers. Although they are well known and respected in other areas, they are not major computer manufacturers. According to a 1983 Future Computing study, three companies split half the personal computer market: IBM with 21%, Radio Shack with 16%, and Apple with 13%. The other 50% is divided by a large number of companies, none of which has more than 5% of the marketplace.

What is a Microcomputer?

A microcomputer can be defined as a computer system that has the following characteristics:

1. It is mass marketed.
2. It can store data on either a diskette or cassette.
3. It can do a variety of tasks such as game playing, word processing, and stock analysis instead of just one dedicated task.
4. It can be programed in either Basic or another computer language.
5. The price for a basic system including computer, video monitor, and one or two disk drives is less than $5000.

Differences Among Microcomputers

The five main differences among microcomputers are as follows:

1. The amount of memory available and at what cost.
2. The type of keyboard.
3. The video display.
4. The storage capabilities.
5. The interfaces available.

Memory

The advertised memory of each computer is usually the most fraudulent point in computer advertising. Every manufacturer makes claims about the total memory available on its machine. What they (and the sales clerks) do not tell you is (1) trying to compare raw memory among different machines is like comparing apple and oranges, and (2) after all advertising claims are compared, each machine, in each class of computer, has nearly the same identical amounts of memory available as any other.

Today's microcomputer comes with between 16 and 64 kilobytes of memory. A kilobyte is 1,024 bytes. The best analogy to a byte is a letter or number. Thus, a computer with 16 kilobyte (or 16 K, as it is normally called) can hold more than 16,000 letters.

Usually, it is only the total amount of memory that is mentioned. What is not mentioned or stressed is the difference between ROM (read-only memory) and RAM (random-access memory). ROM is the memory used to control the computer itself. It tells the computer video how to work, how to read a diskette, how to work the printer, and the like. It cannot be changed. RAM is the amount of space available for your use. It is like a chalkboard that can be wiped clean when you are done with it and used again. The difference between two machines may not be as great as the advertisements.

> Example 2-1: The Commodor 64 is advertised as having 64K of RAM. But its "system specifications" state that only "39K are user-accessible for BASIC programs." This is only 1 K RAM more than is available in a 48K Radio Shack TRS-80 Model III after the disk operating system (DOS) is loaded in.

Always ask how the memory is used. Some computers use their internal memory to control peripherals (e.g., disk drives), whereas others have microprocessors and memory systems built into each peripheral. This difference is important for two reasons. First, if the computer does not know how to work the disk drive, you cannot buy generic, nonintelligent peripherals. You may have to buy the peripherals made by the computer's manufacturer (at a higher price, of course). Second, you will constantly be buying the same thing over and over again. Every time you buy a new peripheral, another microprocesser and memory system is bought. If the computer itself could control the peripheral, you would save the price of the microprocessor and memory system each time you bought another peripheral.

Any specific computer can be sold with different amounts of memory. The sales pitch is that you do not have to pay for excess memory until you "actually" need it. When you need more memory, you take the computer in, and for a price, more memory is added. *Do not fall for this sales pitch!* Before you buy, find out the cost of upgrading memory. An additional 16K of memory can cost between $20 and $400. The difference arises from how the memory is increased. In some machines (for example, Apple and TRS-80) you merely plug additional memory chips into a preexisting circuit board. On other computers (for example, IBM PC) you must buy a memory board with control circuits that are inserted into slots in the computer. Since the board costs more than the bare chips, your cost is higher.

Do not fall for advertising claims that one computer is better than another because it has more memory. Program capabilities are very similar among different brands of microcomputers. What you can do with one machine can usually be done with another. You can have all the memory in the world, but it is not worth the price of a glass of water without the software you need. Never pick one brand of microcomputer because it has more memory than another.

Hint: If you just want to play games or learn how to program without using a disk drive (see the section on storage later in this chapter), 16K of memory is sufficient. If you want to use a disk drive, you must have a minimum of 32K because the disk operating system (DOS) can use a large amount of memory when it is loaded into memory. If you plan to use the computer in business applications, buy as much memory as your particular brand will hold.

Keyboard Types

Keyboard variation is the most ignored difference among computers. Three types of keyboard are available: the plastic membrane, the calculator style, and the typewriter style.

The least desirable keyboard is made of a plastic membrane. It has no moving parts and is entirely electronic in operation. Every time you strike a "key" you close an electric contact. This keyboard is commonly used on lower-priced game computers such as the Timex 1000 and the Atari 400.

The keyboard made of plastic membrane limits what you can do. Theoretically, you can do anything on it; in reality, you cannot. You cannot touch-type on it. If you try, your fingers will quickly get sore and tired. Unless you forcefully strike each key, you take the risk that the key will not register. Membrane keyboards are commonly used on touch-sensitive home appliances such as microwave ovens.

The next most commonly used keyboard type resembles a home calculator. It differs from the membrane keyboard in that each key is raised and works mechanically. But as with the membrane keyboard, unless you forcefully strike each key, it will not register. You cannot touch-type on this keyboard, either. Also it normally has smaller keys than does the typewriter style of keyboard.

The best keyboard to use resembles a typewriter. When you hit a key, you move a mechanical part. It is the most reliable type of keyboard and the easiest to use over long periods. A major difference among the typewriter style of keyboards is the availability of a numeric keypad. This is a separate set of keys that have the numerals 0 to 9, the decimal point, and a key to tell the computer to enter the data. Some computers come with the numeric keypad, some without, and on some it is an option at extra cost. If you plan to do a lot of numeric inputting, this keypad is a must.

Warning: There is no set size for computer keys. The cheaper the computer, the smaller the keys. With small keys, if you have big stubby fingers, you will constantly strike two keys when you meant to hit only one.

Warning: There is no set keyboard layout. Although the major keys, the letters, and the numbers are in the same place, the secondary keys can be in different locations.

> *Example 2-2:* The Radio Shack Model III generates the quotation key ['] by typing a [SHIFT] [2]. The IBM PC has a separate key to the right of the [L] key.

If you are a touch typist, you expect the keys always to be in the same place. If they are in different locations, you will constantly make typing mistakes. This problem arises only if you type on two different keyboards.

Video Displays

The type of computer you buy determines the video display you need. Some computers, such as the Northstar Advantage, Commodore Pet, and Radio Shack TRS-80 Model III, come with a full-sized video display built in. Other computers, such as the Osborne and Otrona Attache, have a tiny built-in monitor (5 by 5 inches on the Osborne). Finally, some computers, such as the Apple II/e, the Atari 800, the IBM PC, and the VIC 20, require you to provide your own video monitor.

Warning: A tiny built-in screen may be hard to read. Once I was testing a new brand of portable computer. The salesman and I looked at the instructions on the screen and hit the letter [D] to open a file. It did not work. After five tries we opened up the manual and learned that we were supposed to hit the letter [O]. Because of the size of the letter as displayed on the tiny screen, we could not tell the difference between the [D] and [O].

There is no universal standard for computer video monitors. What you can get is limited solely by your needs and what you can afford. A video monitor can be in black and white, color, or monochromatic (e.g., a green monitor). You can buy a dedicated monitor (good only as a monitor), or you can use a television set as a monitor.

Television Set.   A television set is the cheapest method of getting a video monitor. A video modulator is attached to the back of your television, and the computer's video output is now displayed on it. When not using the computer, you simply flip a switch and you can watch television.

Warning: If you already have cable television or a video tape recorder, you may not be able to attach the computer's video modulator. Ask before buying.

Dedicated Video Monitor.   A dedicated video monitor is basically a television set that receives only the signal wired into it. It is built to do only one job and it does it well.

Video monitors differ from television sets in that they can come in monochromatic colors; that is, all the letters or symbols appear to be green or orange on a dark background. A black and white monitor has white letters on a black background. The difference is important especially if you spend long times at the computer. There are scientific studies showing it is easier to read a green or orange screen than a black and white screen.

Color vs. Black and White/Monochromatic: No matter how your computer is designed, it can work with a black and white or monochromatic monitor. Buying a color monitor has no advantages for word processing, stock analysis, data base management, and the like. With the cost difference between a 9-inch color and a 9-inch monochromatic monitor being as much as $500, there is no reason to buy a separate color monitor. Too many color monitors are bought solely because a child wants to play a video game in color the way it appears at the video arcade. If a salesperson tries to sell you a color monitor, ask him or her to give you 10 good reasons why a color monitor is better for your purposes than a monochromatic monitor. Remember, the salesperson's job is to get you to spend. The more you spend, the more he or she makes.

What Kind of Monitor to Buy.   If you buy a game microcomputer, either attach it to your present television or buy a new small black and white television (starting as low as $79) to use. If you later decide to give up the computer, you still have a television set.

If you buy a personal computer and will use it for serious purposes or be looking at the screen for long period of time, buy a dedicated monochromatic (not black and white) monitor.

Differences Among Dedicated Monitors.   There are two major differences among most dedicated monitors. First, does the monitor shield you against unnecessary X-rays? Although the video monitor manufacturers claim there is no danger, independent studies are now being conducted to confirm their claims, and the results are not in. For an extra $5 or $10, you can buy a shielded monitor. Second, examine the monitor's antiglare capability. Glare is caused by another light source hitting the video screen, which makes the screen hard to read. For an extra $5 to $25 you can either get anti-glare capabilities built in or get an anti-glare screen that fits over the monitor.

Video Width and Case Ability.   Not all video displays are created equal. Apart from the monitor, the computer itself controls the video width, case ability, and the number of lines per video screen.

Video width determines many characters the computer can generate on its standard line. The number ranges from 22 to 80 per line. This difference determines what applications and what software you can run on the machine.

Video width means nothing to a game computer used primarily for the game cartridges. The game designer takes the video width into consideration when designing the game. The difference becomes important when trying to do "serious" applications, as is shown in the Figure 2-1 on page 17.

Some video displays cannot generate lower case letters even though the computer recognizes them. Compare the following two sentences:

1. The quick brown fox jumped over the moon and sat on the red bed.
2. THE QUICK BROWN FOX JUMPED OVER THE MOON AND SAT ON THE RED BED.

It is easier to read a sentence composed of upper and lower case letters than a sentence of only upper case letters. Also, with only upper case letters, you are limited in what you can do with the computer. Do not even try word processing. If you have a printer attached, you will quickly discover that your printouts are composed of upper and lower case letters in random positions. This happens because some computers internally recognize that you hit the key sequence for a lower case letter (e.g., on some computers a [shift] [letter] key). You cannot see it on the screen. This makes it very difficult to debug programs because some computers cannot accept a command that consists of both upper and lower case letters:

> *Example 2-3:* You see the following line on the screen: "100 PRINT X." The computer sees it as "100 PriNt X." The computer will respond that there is an error in line 100, yet you will not see it.

Just because a computer comes with one standard line length or case does not mean it is "stuck" with that length or case. With some computers, you can add additional computer boards that change the video width. This becomes important when comparing prices and models.

FIGURE 2-1

```
A 64 character line:

---------1---------2---------3---------4---------5---------6---4

        This and the next paragraph are based on 64 characters per
line.   With a maximum of 64 characters, any word that extends
over the edge of the line gets "wrapped-around" and the right
margain is not even.
        Most people, when they type, use 60-64 characters per line.
This line width shows you where your left and right margains will
break.


A 40 character line:

---------1---------2---------3---------4
         0         0         0         0
        This and the following paragraph
are based on a 40 character line.  As
with a 64 character line, any word that
extends over the edge of the line gets
"wrapped around."
        If 40 character screen width is
printed out on a 60-64 character line,
you will not know where the left and
right margains are.


A 22 character line:

---------1---------2-2

        This and the
following paragraph
are based on 22
characters per line.
Notice that even a
short sentence takes
up a number of lines.
        Think how hard
it will be to do word
processing and other
applications that
require a wide video
screen such as a
spreedsheet or data
base management.
```

Example 2-4: An Apple II+ with a monochromatic monitor and the TRS-80 Model III, both with one disk drive, are very close in price. The TRS-80 has a 64-character upper and lower case screen. The Apple II has a 40-character upper case only video display. For an additional $379, you can get a board that plugs into the Apple and lets it display an 80-character upper/lower case video display.

Add the price of the additional board into your computations, and the Apple becomes more expensive.

The final difference deals with the number of lines of information the video screen can generate at one time. The usual range is between 13 and 40. This difference does not make that much difference to the skilled programmer.

Warning: CP/M is a very popular computer operating system in part. Its popularity arises because, theoretically, a CP/M program written on one machine will work on any machine capable of operating CP/M without modification. Hence, many companies are manufacturing CP/M modification boards. What you are not told is that for most CP/M programs to work properly, a screen that is 80-characters wide and has 24 lines is required. Although the CP/M program runs on the machine, its video display is messed up.

Storage Capabilities

Other than constantly retyping a program, there are two methods of storing information and data: cassette and disk.

Cassette.   A cassette system for loading and storing information is typically provided in all microcomputers. Even the IBM PC has a cassette capability.

The only advantage a cassette has over a disk is that it is cheaper. It is an unreliable and slow method of accessing data. If you use a cassette, you may have the dubious pleasure of trying to load a program five or six times before it loads properly. A program that takes five minutes to load by cassette can take 15 seconds by diskette.

With a cassette, there is no reason to use high fidelity cassettes, but then again do not buy the "4 for $1" specials.

Warning: If you must use a cassette, ascertain if you can use any cassette recorder or whether you must use the one built by the computer manufacturer. The one made by the computer manufacturer is much more expensive than the generic recorder.

Disk Drive.   All microcomputers, except for the very inexpensive game machines, have the ability to use a disk drive. A disk drive by itself costs anywhere from $300 on up. To add the first disk drive to a microcomputer typically costs $600 because, in addition to the drive, additional control circuitry must be installed that allows the computer to control the drive.

When buying disk drives there are two main criteria to consider: compatibility and capacity.

Never buy a disk drive on the basis of price alone. First, you must make sure that the disk drive will work on your computer under your specifications (see Example 3-20 for an instance of disk drive incompatibility).

Disk drives come in a variety of configurations. There are single-sided and dual-sided drives; there are single-, dual-, and quad-density disk drives; there are 40-track and 80-track drives.

A single-sided disk drive can put data on only one side of the diskette, whereas a dual-sided disk drive can put information on both sides. An 80-track drive can hold twice as much data as a 40-track drive. Double-density packs the data closer together. It is cheaper to buy one double-density disk drive than two single-density drives. Similarly, it is cheaper to buy one double-sided disk drive than two single-sided drives. Some computers can use any of the variations mentioned, whereas others can use only a specific type.

Warning: Many companies advertise very "low" prices for disk drives. Mentioned in the small print is that these prices do not include a power supply or cabinet, both of which are needed.

Two sizes of disk drives are currently available to the end consumer. One uses a 5¼-inch diskette, and the other uses an 8-inch diskette. Some computers can use either size, whereas others can use only one. The 8-inch diskette can store almost three times as much data as a 5¼-inch diskette.

Warning: In the early days of disk drives, 80-track drives were notorious for not working. The tracks are placed so close together that the slightest misalignment of the drive's recording head causes the drive to be unable to read the diskette. Some experts feel that the newer 80-track drives do not have this problem, but others feel that it still exists.

Hint: If the computer will be used for serious purposes other than playing games and learning how to program, buy a disk drive. The speed and reliability of loading data are worth it.

Save Money: There is a tremendous marketing effort by diskette manufacturers to try to convince you to buy their brand of diskette. This advertising tries to convince you to pay a premium price for a particular brand. The manufacturers claim that you will have less trouble if you use their brand. *Do not fall for this advertising.* The vast majority of quality complaints about diskettes are ultimately resolved by getting the disk drive fixed. Some companies claim their brand is worth a premium price because the data will not be lost. With the typical retail cost per diskette ranging from $2 to $6, you would be safer to make one original and two backups on a $2 diskette than to keep only one original on a $6 diskette. Compare a diskette to gasoline. Although some cars work better on one brand than another, it really does not matter usually what brand you use. *Buy the cheapest brand that works for you.* The same is true of diskettes.

Interfaces

Interfaces are the means by which your computer talks to peripherals such as disk drivers, printers, and communications devices. The more you have, the better off you are. At a minimum, you should have interfaces to attach a printer, disk drives, cassettes, video monitor (unless the computer comes with one), and a modem.

When you check out interfaces, make sure they are either a RS-232 serial port, IEEE 488 port, or a Centronics parallel port. These are the "standard" interface ports. If you get a computer that has its own special type of interface, you will have trouble getting peripherals to work.

Hint: An easy way to check out the interface type is to find out what disk drives, printers, and so on will work with the microcomputer. If only the manufacturer's own brand will work, then you know that the interface is of a non-standard type.

Types of Microcomputers

All microcomputers fall into three categories: game computers, personal computers, and business computers. Some manufacturers make a number of microcomputers with a different machine for each category.

Game Computers

The name, *game computer*, is self-explanatory. Although the manufacturers might claim otherwise, such computers are primarily designed for playing video arcade games. The three common denominators of a game computer are:

1. Type of keyboard.
2. Video screen width.
3. A slot for plugging in game cartridges.

The game keyboard typically has a membrane or calculator type of keyboard. It comes without any video. You are told to wire it to your home television set. The video width is under 40 characters, and the computer cannot generate lower case letters. The game computer has a cartridge slot built in to accept ROM cartridges that contain video arcade games and computer programs.

If you want to use a game microcomputer for a serious purpose such as stock analysis or word processing, be prepared to write your own software. Very little serious software is written for these machines other than those that are written by the computer's manufacturer.

Game microcomputers are usually limited to less than 32K of memory. They are limited to one or two disk drives, some cannot use disk drives at all.

Typical game microcomputers include the Commodore VIC-20, the TRS-80 Color Computer, Texas Instruments' TI-99/4A, and the Atari 400. The average cost is under $400.

Warning: Many third-party sources are selling peripherals designed to upgrade the game computer to a higher level. *Do not buy these peripherals.* Although it is possible to upgrade some of the computer's capabilities, you can never make it truly equal to a personal or business microcomputer; a game computer was built for one essential purpose, to play games. If you own a game computer, you would be better off to sell or junk it and buy a computer that was designed for personal or business computing.

Personal Computers

The personal computer is designed for individual and small business use. It can easily be used for word processing, stock analysis, spreadsheets, and the like. It has a maximum of 64K memory and allows you to access four 5¼-disk drives. Its video width is between 40 and 80 characters, and it can generate upper and lower case letters. It has a typewriter style keyboard.

A full range of software is available for a personal computer. It is as equally at home playing games as it is word processing.

Typical personal computers include the Apple II/e, the Atari 800, the IBM PC, the Heath Z89, and the TRS-80 Model III. Expect to pay around $2000 for a personal computer that includes a video monitor and one or two disk drives.

Business Microcomputers

A business computer is bigger than a personal computer. It is primarily designed for business use, and it would be overkill to have one for home use. A business computer has 128K+ of memory available, can access 8-inch diskettes, and can use CP/M-based software. Business computers are more likely to be designed for one purpose. Some are better at numerical analysis or word processing than others. If you are not careful, you can buy the wrong type. If, for example, you need to access certain data bases such as LEXIS (a legal data base), you must use a business computer.

Brands include Digital Electronic's Rainbow 100, Apple's Lisa, the TRS-80 Model 12, the Hewlett-Packard, and the Wang. Costs range from $4000 to over $15,000.

Peripheral Considerations

There are a variety of peripheral devices that can greatly increase the benefit (and cost) of owning a computer. Peripheral devices are separate from the computer, but they act in conjunction with it. They are also commonly called input/output devices. Besides the disk drive discussed earlier, the two most common peripherals are printers and modems.

Modem

A modem is a device that allows your computer to talk to another computer. It converts your computer's electrical signals into tones that can be transmitted through the telephone system. If you want to access data bases such as CompuServe, The Source, or Dow Jones News/ Retrieval, you must have a modem.

There are two types of modems: the acoustical and the direct connect.

The Acoustical Modem. The acoustical modem requires you to attach two rubber cups to your telephone handset. The modem hears the sound created by the handset. If you have a nonstandard handset, the acoustical modem will not work. The major disadvantage of an acoustical modem is that it can pick up background noises such as people talking or the radio. This noise will be transmitted to both your computer and the one you are linked to. It can cause your computer to "crash" or generate "garbage" in the middle of whatever you are doing.

The Direct Connect Modem. The direct connect modem connects directly into the telephone wires. You plug the modem's cord into the telephone jack and then plug the telephone into the modem. You can use any single-line telephone with a direct connect modem. The major problem with direct connect modems is that if you do not turn the modem off when you are through using it, your telephone line may not work. This can cause havoc in your household. Friends will think your phone is out of order or that you are long-winded.

Warning: If you use a modem, the telephone company's call waiting service must be disconnected. The "blip" sound the telephone makes when another call is waiting will create garbage on your computer.

A direct connect modem cannot work on a multiline phone system without additional wiring.

Hint: If you will use a modem often, get a dedicated telephone line for it. This will solve two problems. First, you will still have a telephone line available while using the modem. Second, with a dedicated line, you will not be thrown off or get garbage if someone else picks up an extension and says hello.

Printers

Four types of printers are available for microcomputers: thermal, dot matrix, daisy wheel, and plotter. When buying a printer, there are four points you should consider:

1. Price.
2. Print quality.
3. Speed.
4. Ability to print graphics.

Thermal Printers.   A thermal printer is the cheapest type available, with an average cost of less than $500. It prints by "burning" the image onto specially treated paper. It rarely prints more than 50 characters per second. Its print fades when exposed to sunlight. Thermal printers are rarely used today in stand-alone printers.

Dot Matrix Printers.   A dot matrix printer prints by having a series of tiny wires strike the paper. The letters they make are composed of tiny dots. The more wires there are, the closer the dots, and the better the letter looks. Prices range from $300 to over $5000. Speed ranges from 50 to 500 characters per second. When looking at a dot matrix printer, find out if it descends lower case letters. Certain lower case letters (e.g., "y," "g," and "p") descend below the printing line. Some dot matrix printers cannot descend these letters, and they may look funny to the reader—or downright illegible. See Figure 2-2 on page 24.

FIGURE 2-2

$400 PRINTER

```
0123456789:-ABCDEFGHIJKLMNOPQRSTUVWXYZabcdefghjijklmnoPqrstuvwx
z!"#$%&'()@*\[]^~!()_)0123456789:-ABCDEFGHIJKLMNOPQRSTUVWXYZabcd
fghjijklmnoPqrstuvwxyz!"#$%&'()@*\[]^~!()
```

$800 PRINTER

```
0123456789:-ABCDEFGHIJKLMNOPQRSTUVWXYZabcdefghjijklmnopqrstuvwx
z!"#$%&'()@*\[]^~!{0123456789:-ABCDEFGHIJKLMNOPQRSTUVWXYZabcd
fghjijklmnopqrstuvwxyz!"#$%&'()@*\[]^~!{}
```

$1200 PRINTER

```
0123456789:-ABCDEFGHIJKLMNOPQRSTUVWXYZabcdefghjijklmnopqrstuvw
xyz!"#$%&'()@*\[ ]^~!()0123456789:-ABCDEFGHIJKLMNOPQRSTUVWXYZa
bcdefghjijklmnopqrstuvwxyz!"#$%&'()@*\[ ]^~!()
```

$1600 printer

```
0123456789:-ABCDEFGHIJKLMNOPQRSTUVWXYZabcdefghjijklmnopqrstuvwx
z!"#$%&'()@*\[ ]^~!0123456789:-ABCDEFGHIJKLMNOPQRSTUVWXYZabcd
fghjijklmnopqrstuvwxyz!"#$%&'()@*\[ ]^~!()
```

$2000 printer

```
0123456789:-ABCDEFGHIJKLMNOPQRSTUVWXYZabcdefghjijklmnopqrstuvw
xyz!"#$%&'()@*\[]^~!{}0123456789:-ABCDEFGHIJKLMNOPQRSTUVWXYZab
cdefghjijklmnopqrstuvwxyz!"#$%&'()@*\[]^~!{}
```

Some dot matrix printers can print graphic symbols or generate a wide variety of type faces. For example, the Epson MX-80 printer used with the right software can print in italic, Old English, and script typefaces. See Figure 2-3 on page 25. If you have a program that allows you to draw a picture on the video screen, the printer can print the picture onto paper.

Daisy Wheel Printers. A daisy wheel printer is commonly called of "letter quality." It can generate clear crisp letters that look typewritten. If a character is not on the print wheel, it cannot be generated. Specialized print wheels are available in a wide variety of typefaces including scientific notation, Spanish, Greek, plus numerous English type faces. The only danger with print wheels is that one character in a certain place on one print wheel can be an entirely different character in the same place on another wheel. For example:

> The following phrase was composed on a Lexitron VT-1303 using a Qume printer with a Courier 10 print wheel: "[state your name]." When the print wheel was replaced with a Bookface Academic 10, the phrase was printed "μstate your nameβ".

ABCDEFGHIJKLMNOPQRSTUVWXYZ
1234567890:!"£$%&'()* °+;/?.,

ABCDEFGHIJLMNOPQRSTUVWXYZ
abcdefghijklmnopqrstuvwxyz
1234567890:!"#$%¢'()*@+;/?.,<>

ABCDEFGHIJLMNOPQRSTUVWXYZ
abcdefghijklmnopqrstuvwxyz
1234567890:!"#$%&'[ ]* +;/?.,‹

The speed of letter-quality printers ranges from 7 to 55 characters per second. Price ranges from $700 to $3500.

Warning: Many companies are selling converted electric typewriters as printers. Their selling point is that you can have a letter-quality printer at a fraction of the normal letter-quality printer price, plus the capability of a full typewriter if you need it (helpful in filling out forms, etc). Do not buy one. They are designed for "light" computer use and frequently break down. They are not built to take the continuous typing that a computer generates. If you do not want to have a separate letter-quality printer and a typewriter, buy a letter-quality printer that has a keyboard attached (normally $3000 to $4000). They differ from the converted electric typewriters in that they are printers modified to be typewriters instead of typewriters modified to be printers.

Plotter Printers. The final type of printer is called a plotter. It is a highly specialized printer which can draw bar charts, pie charts, and the like. See Figure 2-4 on pages 26 and 27. Although it can draw

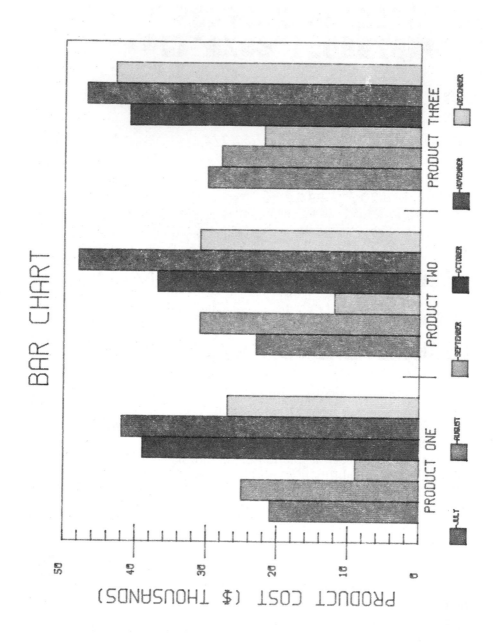

26

PIE CHARTS CAN CLARIFY IN COLOR!

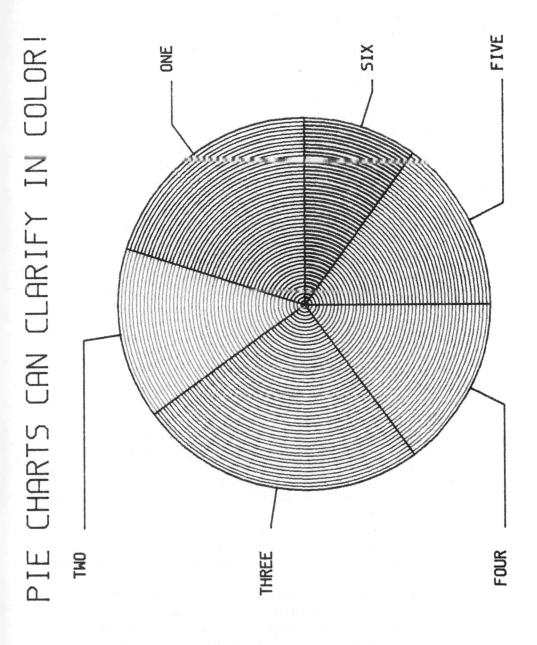

ONE

SIX

FIVE

TWO

THREE

FOUR

beautiful charts, do not use it for word processing. If you have a document that contains both text and a chart, two separate documents will have to be printed. First, you will have to print either the text or the chart. Then you must disconnect that printer and attach the other; print the second document; then disconnect the second printer and reattach the first printer.

Specific Recommendations About Printers. The type of printer you get should depend on the work you need to do. Unless you need to write business letters and the like, get a good quality dot matrix printer that can print graphics.

CARRIAGE WIDTH: When buying a printer, get one with a wide carriage. Some printers have a 9½-inch carriage whereas others are 16 inches wide. A 9½-inch carriage can typically print an 80-character wide line, and a 16-inch carriage can print 140 characters. You may not need 140 characters in the beginning, but if you need it, it is available. If you buy a 9½-inch carriage printer and need a 140-character line printed out, you will have to get another printer.

FRICTION FEED VS. TRACTOR/PIN FEED: There are two different ways to hold the paper in a printer: friction and tractor/pin feed. Friction feed is what is used in typewriters. Friction between the platen and feed rollers holds the paper in place. Tractor/pin feed requires the use of continuous feed paper. You place the holes on the continuous feed in the tractor feed. When the platen moves, the tractor moves, which in turn moves the paper. Pin feed differs from tractor in that the pins are built into the platen. They are not adjustable; you cannot use them to hold papers of different sizes. A tractor feed is usually an add-on feature that can add $250 to the cost of the printer. The tractor feed is adjustable so that it can use a variety of different size papers.

You do not need a tractor feed unless you use continuous feed paper. If you are willing to feed the paper to the printer one sheet at a time, you can use friction feed.

Warning: If you think you will need a tractor feed, make sure it is available; the cheaper the printer, the greater the likelihood that no tractor feed is made for it.

Warning: Some programs assume you are using continuous feed paper. They do not stop at the end of each page and wait for you to add another sheet. If you use continuous feed paper without a tractor or pin feed in such a situation, the paper will "walk" over the platen. Eventually the printer will be printing on the platen and not the paper.

PRINTER SUPPLIES: Do not buy a printer without having a ready source of ribbons and other supplies available. Many dealers will gladly sell you the printer, but they do not keep spare ribbons in stock because there is not enough profit.

PRINTER SPEED: Get the fastest printer you can afford. Take the following bench marks. Assume a page of 64-character lines, with 50 lines printed per page. At seven characters per second, it takes seven minutes to print a page; at 45 characters per second, it takes a little more than one minute; at 200 characters per second, it takes under 15 seconds. If you are using your printer for business, time is money. If you have to print an occasional business letter, consider getting two printers: a cheap letter quality printer that prints at seven characters per second for letters and a high-speed dot matrix printer for your other uses.

PRINTABLE CHARACTERS: Another important difference among printers is their capability to print certain unique characters. The cheaper printers can generate only those letters, numbers, and symbols found on the keyboard. The more expensive printers can print a wide variety of unique characters, such as TM, ¶, ®, §, ©, °, £, Y, {, }, ~, ç μ, é, ¢, β, and ½.

PRINTER CAPABILITIES: The more expensive the printer, the greater the capabilities built into it. These abilities may include printing

FIGURE 2-5

Printer Capabilities

Not all printers have the same capability. Some can print **boldface**, some can <u>underline</u>, and some can even <u>double underline</u>.

Most printers can print in a single or double spaced mode. There is none or only one blank line between text. Some printers can print in $\frac{1}{2}$ line increments. Instead of having just one line between text, you can have $1\frac{1}{2}$ or $2\frac{1}{2}$ between lines.

This ability can be especially important when preparing speeches or rough drafts where you plan to do extensive editing.

Other Important Features

If you prepare newsletters, you will want a printer that can do a reverse form feed and generate columns like this example.

If you do scholarly research, you will want a printer that can easily print subscripts and superscripts.

You may want to put footnotes in your text. For example, "According to Gilmore's article on Transborder Data Regulation[1], the EEC will sharply limit imports of personal computers."

On the other hand you may want to print in scientific notation:

$$R = E^{\frac{1}{2}} (Z^{23} M \cdot_{z-1} * L_{n-1} / (-T^x_r - V1) * W_a)$$

superscripts and subscripts; printing in half, one, two, and three line increments; doing a reverse form feed and printing in columns; printing underlines and boldface; and finally achieving true proportional spacing. See Figure 2-5 on page 29.

Warning: Unknowing sales persons confuse proportional spacing with justified right margin. In proportional spacing the letter "w" will take up more space than the letter "i." This is different from typing in pica, which has 10 characters to the inch, or typing in elite, which has 12 characters to the inch. Do not let a salesperson tell you that having that right margin justified is the same as proportional spacing. The easiest way to tell the difference between the two is that when the right margin is justified, the gaps are between the words, and in proportional spacing, the gaps are between the letters.

You can see this difference in Figure 2-6 on this page.

FIGURE 2-6

Proportional Spaced, Justified:

We the People of the United States, in order to form a more perfect Union, Establish Justice, insure domestic Tranquility, provide for the common defense, promote the General Welfare, and secure the Blessing of Liberty to ourselves and our Posterity, do ordain and establish this Constitution for the United States of America.

Mono Spaced, Justified:

We the People of the United States, in order to form a more perfect Union, Establish Justice, insure domestic Tranquility, provide for the common defense, promote the General Welfare, and secure the Blessing of Liberty to ourselves and our Posterity, do ordain and establish this Constitution for the United States of America.

Software

A personal computer is worthless without software to operate it. Unfortunately *most* software currently available is worthless. The following paragraphs offer some specific suggestions to keep in mind when buying software:

1. *See before you buy.* Be sure the software is available. The microcomputer industry is notorious for promising delivery of software in the near future. Many times you will be told that the software will be released any day now. Too often, promised delivery dates are never kept.

2. *Use the software and manual before you buy it.* Most stores will gladly demonstrate the software for you. Some software packages even have demonstration modules built in. *This is wrong.* You would not let a car salesman test drive the automobile for you, so why should the salesperson test the program for you? Let the salesperson run the demonstration, but then sit down with the manual and try a few features yourself. You cannot expect to become an instant expert, but you should get a feel for the program and documentation. If you have trouble understanding or getting a simple function to work then, think what will happen when you get to the complicated features.

If a vendor will not open a package and allow you to try out the software to your heart's content, go someplace else.

3. *Buy integrated packages.* Software is complicated. It is better to buy one expensive program that does many things than to buy 10 inexpensive programs that do only one small thing each. Never buy two programs when one program will suffice.

> *Example 2-5:* Many mailing list programs are available. However, a good data base management program can do the same job if the fields are properly defined.

Buy software packages that can "talk" to one another.

> *Example 2-6:* Radio Shack's SuperScripsit word processing program can extract information from Visicalc and Profile III Plus programs. You can use SuperScripsit to generate form letters from the mailing list you maintain on Profile III+.

> *Example 2-7:* AlphaBit Communication's Lazy Writer word processing program can internally call and use Cornucopia Software's Electric Webster Dictionary program. When the dictionary has finished proofing a document, you are automatically returned to the document.

If you could not call Electric Webster from Lazy Writer, you would have to exit Lazy Writer; run Electric Webster; quit Electric Webster when it was done; run Lazy Writer; and load the corrected document into Lazy Writer.

4. *Examine documentation before you buy.* If possible (and it is not always possible), buy and examine the manual before you buy the underlying software. If a company has only a 15-page mimeographed manual, and the program costs $300, you know something is wrong. The more expensive the program, the better the documentation should be.

One way to compare software documentation is to see how much handholding there is. Does the documentation have a lot of examples? Does it simply explain things, or does it refer you all over the manual? Are there pictures of how the screen looks at various stages?

> *Example 2-8:* Profile III Plus was written for Radio Shack by the small [sic] Computer Company. The manual sold with the program by small is less than 100 pages. The manual sold by Radio Shack is over 200 pages.

5. *Buy assembly language programs.* Assembly or machine language programs run much faster than programs written in an interpretive language (such as BASIC). You will appreciate the speed, especially after you wait one hour for the program to sort 600 names.

6. *Do not buy software that cannot be duplicated.* Some companies sell software that you cannot duplicate (backed-up) or that limits the number of duplications to one or two. Their purpose is to discourage you from giving copies to your friends. Their goals may be understandable, but their actions are not.

What are you to do when the master diskette or cassette "dies" and you need to run the program? The company will say, "Send us the diskette/cassette and we will send you a replacement." They do not care if you cannot use the program until you get the replacement. Think of the problems that would result if a business could not access its data. If you were an employee, how would you feel if the boss says, "Mary, I am sorry, but I cannot pay you today. The payroll computer program was damaged, and we need to get a new master copy to print the check." Also consider the problem that would arise if the software company later went out of business.

Warning: If you must buy protected software, do not buy it on cassette. The tape wears out much faster than the magnetic media on a diskette.

7. Be wary if a retailer sells you complex software (anything other than a game) without a warranty or registration card. Software piracy is so rampant that authors and publishers will support only registered owners. Some have even put time locks into their programs that require you to contact them. If you are not registered, you get no support.

Final Software Comment

The preceding suggestions notwithstanding, the most important thing is for the software to fulfill your needs. Sometimes software violates all the rules but can actually be more suited to your needs than one that follows the rules.

Take the following facts. I had a mailing list of 600 names. The names were entered into the file in random order. The information contained first name, last name, street, city, and state as shown in the four examples listed below:

1. John Small, 12 Jackson St., Kalamin, Michigan.
2. David Small, POB 1243, Kalamin, Michigan.
3. Maria Davidson, 202 Main Street, Jackson, Nevada.
4. Ken Johnson, 56 Jackson Lane, Portland, Alabama.

I had the information on two different data base programs. The first was written in assembly language. It could be interfaced with other programs. It was very fast and could sort 600 names in less than 30 seconds. But it could not sort multiple fields; it could sort on only one key:

By last name:
3. Maria Davidson, 202 Main Street, Jackson, NV
4. Ken Johnson, 56 Jackson St., Portland, AL;
1. John Small, 12 Jackson St., Kalamin, MI;
2. David Small, POB 1243, Kalamin, MI.

By state:
4. Ken Johnson, 56 Jackson St., Portland, AL;
1. John Small, 12 Jackson St., Kalamin, MI;
2. David Small, POB 1243, Kalamin, MI;
3. Maria Davidson, 202 Main Street, Jackson, NV.

No matter how the file was sorted, John Small would always come before David Small. The program could *not* sort first by state, then last name, and then first name.

The second program was written in Basic. It could not talk to other programs. It was not as versatile as the first program. It took 45 minutes to sort 600 names. Yet it could sort on multiple fields. First it could sort by state, then last name, and finally first name.

By state, last name, and first name:
4. Ken Johnson, 56 Jackson St., Portland, AL;
2. David Small, POB 1243, Kalamin, MI;
1. John Small, 12 Jackson St., Kalamin, MI;
3. Maria Davidson, 202 Main St., Jackson, NV.

Thus, although the first program was "better" because it fulfilled the rules, the second actually fulfilled my needs better.

The Law of Sales

3

The American law of sales arose out of the early decisions of English judges in solving the disputes of the English mercantile class. These decisions were transplanted to the New World by the colonists and expanded by American judges. As the United States grew, so did the laws of sales.

The United States law of sales remained judge-made until the late nineteenth century when an attempt was made to codify it. At that time, the amount of commercial business across state lines was increasing. No longer were the vast majority of business transactions between a local merchant and his local customer. National growth required that a uniform set of laws and understandings be reached.

To appreciate the need for uniformity, assume one state had a law that said contracts involving more than $200 had to be in writing and another state said that only contracts for more than $100 had to be in writing. Did a contract entered into solely by telephone, involving $150 between residents of the two states have to be in writing? This and similar problems caused the legal community a large amount of grief.

In 1892 the National Conference of Commissioners on Uniform State Laws was formed and started proposing "uniform laws" that would be the same in every state. In 1906 it recommended the "Uniform Sales Act." The Act suffered from one major problem: It was not passed by all the states.

By the 1940s, the National Conference realized that new commercial practices had emerged in the developed United States (as opposed to the developing United States of the 1890s) and established a panel to update and reconcile any inconsistencies among its previously recommended Uniform Laws. Realizing the magnitude of this task, some legal scholars suggested that an entirely new uniform law be drafted that would codify and represent the commercial changes that had occurred in the real world. This suggestion was debated and accepted.

The Uniform Commercial Code (UCC)

Drafting of the Uniform Commercial Code (hereinafter called the UCC) began in 1944. It presently contains nine articles and deals with such things as the law of sales, banking law, secured transactions, negotiable instruments, and the like. Starting with Pennsylvania in 1953, every state, the District of Columbia, Guam, Puerto Rico, and the Virgin Islands have substantially adopted it. This chapter concerns itself only with the law of sales.

The UCC, although covering the law of sales, is not the sole source of sales law. As stated by UCC §1-103, "Unless displaced by the particular provision of [the UCC], the principles of law relative to capacity to contract, principal and agent, . . . , mistake, . . . , or other validity or invalidity cause shall supplement its [i.e., the UCC's] provision." This means that any local state law still controls any point not covered by the UCC. These local points include who has capacity to contract, what constitutes fraud, and so on.

UCC Article 2 codifies the law of sales. It is the law in every American jurisdiction except Louisiana. Except for minor differences among the various states' enactments, it is the same throughout the nation.

Goods versus Services

UCC Article 2 applies only to "goods." It does not apply to "services." UCC §2-105 defines "goods" as follows:

> . . . all things (including specially manufactured goods) which are moveable at the time of identification to the contract for sale other than the money in which the price is to be paid . . .

This definition is much more complex than it appears. Consider the following examples:

1. A sprinkler system is installed in a lawn (*Anderson & Nafziger* vs. *G.T. Newcomb Inc.* (1979, 100 Id. 175, 595 P.2d 709).

2. A photographer is hired to take wedding pictures (*Carpel v. Saget Studios, Inc.*, EDPA, 1971, 326 F. Supp. 1331).
3. An airline ticket and lodging are purchased from a travel agent (*Rosen vs. DePorter-Butterworth Tours, Inc.* (1978, 62 Ill. App. 3rd 762, 379 NE2d 407).
4. A dentist builds a set of dentures (*Preston vs. Thompson* (1981, 53 NC App. 290, 280 SE2d 780).

In the first two examples, the judge ruled that "goods" were involved and that in the last two "services" were involved.

Microcomputer purchases do not present as much trouble. Consider the following three situations:

1. A $100 factory-built memory expansion module is bought and installed by a local store.
2. The unassembled expansion module is bought from a third party, and a local technician is paid $50 to assemble and install it.
3. The unassembled expansion module kit is bought from a local retailer who builds and installs it.

The first situation is clearly a sale of goods, and the second is clearly a sale of services. The third is questionable. One approach used in analyzing the situation is to ask, "What is the *dominant* feature of the transaction?" If the sale of the goods dominates, the transaction is a sale of goods and the UCC applies. If services dominate the transaction, then the UCC does not apply.

Is Software "Goods"?

Whether or not computer software is "goods" has not been finally resolved by the courts. In the early days of computers, software was not considered goods because each implementation included modification to fit each user's needs. There is no clear-cut case stating that software is goods. The closest decision to this premise is a 1978 Federal District Court case, *Triangle Underwriters, Inc. vs. Honeywell, Inc.*, EDNY, 457 F. Supp. 765, where the court ruled that in a "turn-key system" (buyer walks in, turns the key on, and the unit works) software could be classified as goods. As software becomes more prevalent, this trend will grow, but only in respect to "canned" software. If the software is bought "off the shelf" without the expectation of modification (e.g., Visicalc), then it is goods. If it is specially written or modified for a particular end user, then it is a service.

What is a Contract?

Every sales situation involves a contract. The contract consists of an offer to sell or buy and an acceptance of that offer. It exists whether a piece of penny gum or a $50 million jet aircraft is purchased. A contract may be written or oral, express or implied, void or voidable. A contract exists when there is a promise or set of promises for which the law will grant relief if the promise is broken. UCC §1-201 defines a contract as "the total legal obligation which results from the parties' agreement."

In the sale of goods, a contract exists when three criteria have been met:

1. The parties have the capacity to contract.
2. There is an offer.
3. An acceptance of that offer has been made.

Capacity to Contract

In theory, anyone can make a contract with another and agree to any terms he wants, provided he has the capacity to contract. The two groups who do not have the capacity to contract are the mentally infirm and infants. If they enter into a contract, it is either void per se or voidable. The term voidable means that the contract is binding on all the parties until such time as the party without capacity or his guardian decides to disaffirm it.

In the area of microcomputer sales, it is the term infant that causes the problems. The legal definition of infant is very different from the everyday definition. To the law, an infant is an "unemancipated minor." As an unemancipated minor, the infant could buy a microcomputer, take it home, destroy it that night, and legally be entitled to a complete refund the next day.

The rule was made to protect the infant from his own immaturity and the overreaching of "unscrupulous adults."

Years ago, an unemancipated minor would have to reach the age of 21 or join the Armed Forces in order to be held to his or her contracts. This is no longer the general rule. Every American jurisdiction, except Puerto Rico, has lowered the age at which an unemancipated minor can buy goods to eighteen.

What Happens When an Infant Disaffirms Purchases?

A minor can disaffirm his or her purchase and recover any payment made. The only difference among the states is whether the seller can recoup any of the financial loss incurred while the goods were in the infant's possession. The states fall into three main categories: (1) seller gets nothing, (2) seller can recover depreciation, or (3) seller gets fair rental value.

No Recovery.   This is the most popular viewpoint. Absent willful or malicious damage to the property, the infant (remember he can be 17 years and 364 days old) may recover the purchase price without any liability for use, depreciation, damage, or other diminution of value. It does not matter if the sale was for the benefit of the infant or even that the parent or guardian was present when the sale was made.

> *Example 3-1:* A seller sells a $3000 microcomputer to a 17-year-old. During the next year, the infant modifies the computer by drilling holes, replacing memory chips, and so on. He also drops the computer and cracks the computer case. On his eighteenth birthday, he "disaffirms the sale." He is legally entitled to a refund. (See *Halbman* vs. *Lemke*, 1980, 99 Wis.2d 241, 298 NW2d 562.)

Depreciation Recoverable: The second group of states allows an infant to (1) disaffirm his purchases, (2) return the goods, and (3) recover the purchase price or money paid to date minus the amount the property depreciated while the infant possessed it.
    The problem with this approach is determining the amount of depreciation. It is one thing to state the "book value" of a 1980 Chevrolet Caprice; it is quite another to determine the fair market value of an IBM PC microcomputer sold last year. Although there are some studies indicating that the market value of used electronic equipment is anywhere from 40 to 70% of the new retail price, these studies are not universally accepted. Also consider the problem of software.

> *Example 3-2:* What is the depreciated value of a word processing program bought last year when the identical program is still being sold and the original disk, operator's manual, and supporting documentation were returned in brand new condition?

With the software it is arguable that there is no depreciation, and thus the infant is entitled to a full refund.

Fair Rental Value Recoverable: The last group of states allows a seller to recoup the fair rental value of the property from a disaffirming minor. This may not be as good as it sounds.

> *Example 3-3:* An infant buys a computer system on March 1. On March 2, the computer is dropped on a concrete floor. On March 3, the purchase is disaffirmed. What is the fair rental value of the computer for the two days? Compare that to the loss the seller will incur.

What Happens When an Infant Disaffirms a Sale?

An infant can also disaffirm his sales.

> *Example 3-4*: A used expansion module is bought from a 16-year-old for $100. Next year, because of the scarcity of the expansion module, it is now worth $1000. The infant can return the $100 and recover the module.

The only exception to this rule is found in UCC §2-403. If the module was resold to a bona fide purchaser, that sale cannot be voided. The law will protect the innocent purchaser who did not know the seller originally bought the module from an infant.

Practical Considerations

Any seller should be wary of selling expensive equipment to infants. Large sales should be restricted to adults. If an infant wants to buy expensive goods, the seller should require that a parent accompany the infant. The sales ticket should be in the parent's name and not the infant's. With small items, the risk of incurring a loss on any one item may be outweighed by the advantages of making many sales to minors. Finally, realize that for the infant to get his money back, it may be necessary for him to file a lawsuit. Although the seller would probably lose such a suit if it came to trial, he may be able to negotiate a better deal than the law would give him.

What Is An Offer?

An offer is a present promise to do something or refrain from doing something in the future, whether it be the next second or the next year.

> *Example 3-5*: An offer would exist if I said to you "I will sell you my computer for $500" or if you asked me "How much will you sell me your computer for?" and I respond, "$500."

An offer does not exist if one party merely states his intention or gives an opinion.

> *Example 3-6*: I say to you and a group of people, "I am going to sell my computer for $500." You cannot then say "I accept, here is $500, give me the computer." (see *Mellen* vs. *Johnson*, 1948, 322 Mass. 236, 76 NE2d 658.)

The statement indicated only my *future* intention and not my present intention.

This principle holds even if the seller was offered $400 for his computer, and he responded he would not sell for less than $500. A buyer could not tender $500 and expect a court to require the seller to give him the computer. The court will interpret the seller's response as merely saying, "Make me an offer." (see *Owen* vs. *Tunison*, 1932, 131 Me. 42, 158 A. 926.) Judges do not like to find a proposal to be an offer unless there is no other alternative but to find that an offer has been made.

An offer can be revoked by the person making the offer at any time prior to acceptance.

> *Example 3-7:* A merchant puts a sign in his window on Monday with an arrow pointing to a specific computer. The sign reads "Special Demo Sale—This Week Only: $100 for entire system." Nothing prevents him from revoking the offer on Tuesday just as a buyer walks in.

The only exception to this rule is found in UCC §2-205. If a merchant states in writing that the offer will not be revoked, it cannot be revoked for the period of time stated. If no time is stated, it cannot be revoked for a reasonable time, provided that the period of irrevocability cannot exceed three months.

> *Example 3-8:* Buyer sees an advertised item but cannot pay for it now. He writes the merchant seller and asks how long the sale will be in effect. The merchant writes back and states he will sell the product at the advertised price anytime during the next two months. He cannot revoke the offer prior to the end of the two months.

Is an Advertisement an Offer?

Most ethical advertisers intend to fulfill the terms and conditions of their advertisements even if it means a financial loss for them. In those situations where the seller is unable or unwilling to sell the product at the advertised price, there is nothing you can do.

> *Example 3-9:* A local store runs an advertisement offering to sell a famous brand of diskettes at half price. Buyer rushes down to the store, only to discover none are left. There is nothing he can legally do to make the store sell him the diskettes (see *Craft* vs. *Elder & Johnston Co.*, Oh. App. 1941, 38 NE2d 416).

It is possible so many people will want to take advantage of the advertisement that it would be impossible for the seller to have or obtain sufficient stock to fulfill all the orders.

This general rule has two exceptions. First, if a specific quantity is mentioned, the seller must be willing to sell the quantity mentioned.

Example 3-10: Seller advertises in the Sunday newspaper that he will sell one new computer system, normally retailing for $2000, for $100 on a first come, first served basis. You are the very first one at the store the next morning and present your $100. The seller says sorry but no sale. A court will hold that by mentioning the quantity, the merchant made a specific offer that can be accepted. (see *Lefkowitz* vs. *Great Minneapolis Surplus*, 1957, 251 Minn 188, 86 NW2d 689.)

The second exception has already been mentioned in *Example 3-8*— when a merchant seller offers to hold the price open for a firm period not to exceed three months.

Rainchecks

Many times a store will sell out of a product in the middle of a sale. It then issues a "raincheck," which allows the holder to take advantage of the sale price at a later date. A raincheck is an offer that can be revoked at any time by the seller (see *Lowenstein* vs. *Stop & Shop Companies, Inc.*, MA Super. Ct., 10/81, 32 UCCRS 414).

Some states restrict this practice. For example, Ohio's Department of Commerce, Rule 1301:3-3-02(A)(2)(D), states:

> The failure to give rainchecks to consumers after the original quantity of goods is exhausted or the refusal to take orders for the advertised goods or services at the advertised price to be delivered within a reasonable time, unless the supplier has clearly and adequately disclosed the specific quantity of advertised goods or services available [is a deceptive trade practice]; . . .

Check with a state's attorney general or a local consumer group to see if your state has a similar rule.

In those states where there is no rule, the merchant is not obligated to honor the raincheck. Since he was not originally required to sell the goods at the advertised price, he is not required to sell it later at the advertised price. There is a simple way to get around this situation: Put some money down on the purchase ($1 will do) when receiving the raincheck. This way you and the seller have entered into a binding contract to purchase the item at the sale price.

What Is Acceptance?

Prior to the UCC there were highly technical rules on how an offer could be accepted; mail offers could be accepted only by mail, telegraph offers only by telegraph. If a buyer made an offer, the seller had to accept *exactly* what was offered. Any change in conditions or terms was a "counteroffer" and was construed as a *rejection*. Once an offer was rejected, it could not later be accepted without being reoffered.

> *Example 3-11:* A seller offers his computer for $500 cash. Buyer counteroffers with $500 by credit card; the offer has been *rejected*. Buyer cannot later change his mind and accept the offer by offering to pay the $500 cash.

These nitpicking rules were detrimental to commerce and were changed in the UCC. Section 2-206 rejects the formal approach and allows the offeree (the one to whom the offer was made) to accept the offer in any "reasonable" manner.

A written offer can be accepted by telephone. Or if a buyer offers to buy goods and asks for immediate shipment, then shipping constitutes acceptance.

Acceptance and the Battle of the Forms

Many buyers and sellers send acknowledgments of orders. In the acknowledgment, there may be a page of additional terms. Unless you are a merchant in the type of goods being sold, the terms are *not* binding. They are considered to be "proposals for addition to the contract." If you are a merchant dealing with another merchant, these terms will become a part of the contract unless: (1) your original offer expressly limited acceptance to the terms of the original offer, (2) they materially alter it (e.g., they would result in unreasonable surprise or hardship if incorporated into the contract without your being aware of it), or (3) you notify the sender within a reasonable time that you object to the new terms.

> *Merchant Example 3-12:* A merchant buyer orders 100 boxes of diskettes. The seller sends an acknowledgment that states if a dispute arises, it will be settled by binding arbitration.

Unless the merchant buyer objects, the arbitration clause becomes part of the contract.

General Rules

Two common law rules, the "Statute of Frauds" and the "Parol Evidence Rule," are so important to the sale of goods that they have been codified into the UCC.

Statute of Frauds

The Statute of Frauds is one of the oldest rules applicable to the sale of goods, originating in a 1677 Act of the English Parliament. It states what kinds of contracts must be in writing. Its current form can be found in UCC §2-201:

> [A] contract for the sale of goods for the price of five hundred dollars or more is not enforceable by way of action [i.e., lawsuit] or defense unless there is some writing sufficient to indicate that a contract for sale has been made between the parties and signed by the party against whom enforcement is sought or his authorized agent . . .

Without this provision, nothing would prevent a dishonest buyer from getting two witnesses and all three testifying in court that the seller agreed to sell a $10,000 computer for only $1000.

The agreement does not have to be in any particular form. It can be a store receipt, a letter, a check, a telegram, or even a memo written in lead pencil on a scratch pad. The price, time or place of delivery or payment, the general quality of the goods, or any particular warranties may be omitted. It does not have to be signed *per se*; it can have a stamped "signature." All that is wanted is some way to prove that the liable party agreed to the terms.

> *Example 3-13:* A buyer wants a $1000 computer but cannot pay for it. He puts down $5 cash and receives a sales slip with the seller's name preprinted on it and which the sales clerk has initialed. The slip has written on it his name, address, what he purchased, and the total due. When he comes back later, the seller says he will not sell. Since buyer has the sales slip, "signed" by the seller's agent (the sales clerk's initials), it is sufficient to bind the seller. Compare this to a situation in which the buyer does not wish to pay the balance. Since there is nothing to indicate that he signed the sales slip, he cannot be held to the contract. On the other hand, if he had paid the $5 deposit by a credit card, then there is a writing signed by him that refers back to the sales slip. In such a case he could be held liable.

Without something in writing, signed by the person to be held liable, an agreement to purchase a product for more than $500 cannot be enforced.

The Parol Evidence Rule

UCC §2-202 states that when parties put their agreement in writing, any and all previous oral agreements are merged into the written memorandum. No terms in the written contract or agreement can be modified or changed by oral statements unless fraud is alleged.

Example 3-14: A seller's receipt has printed on its face in bold letters the phrase "NO CASH REFUNDS." Before buyer will buy the goods, the sales clerk orally agrees that he may try the product at home for a week; if he does not like it, he can return it for a full refund. Buyer pays for it and takes it home. A week later he returns the unsatisfactory item for a cash refund. He cannot find the sales clerk and speaks with the owner. She refuses and points out the "NO CASH REFUND" printed on the agreement. Buyer is stuck. Had he written down the oral agreement on the sales slip, then the owner would be obligated to refund the money.

Example 3-15: A buyer purchases a used computer for $2000 cash from a merchant. The merchant suggests that to save sales tax the sales slip be written for only $750. The buyer agrees. One week later he discovers the unit has serious hidden defects and demands his money back. The dealer agrees and says, "Here is your $750." Buyer says "No, I gave you $2000 cash." The seller will point to the $750 on your sales ticket and say, "Sue me!" If the matter goes to court, the buyer will have difficulties explaining to the judge why he allowed the wrong amount to be written on the sales ticket.

The Parol Evidence Rule will *not* prohibit a buyer from bringing in additional information, such as documents, to explain a point not covered by the memorandum.

Example 3-16: A used computer is bought from a merchant. The sales slip does not mention warranties. The dealer says the unit was sold "as is," but the buyer says he orally promised a 90-day warranty. The buyer can bring in additional information to prove there was a warranty.

Under the Parol Evidence Rule a party can also bring in additional evidence:

1. To show there was a subsequent agreement altering the original agreement (e.g., seller's sales slip says item was sold "as is." Seller later writes a letter stating there was a 90-day warranty).
2. To prove that the agreement was not to be a contract until the occurrence of some condition.
3. To prove that the agreement is void because of fraud, mistake, duress, and so on.

Integration Clauses

Many sales agreements contain integration clauses. An integration clause means that the entire agreement is contained in the contract and that there is no other agreement outside the contract.

Sample Text: Customer acknowledges by its signature that it has read both sides of this AGREEMENT, understands it and that it constitutes the

FIGURE 3-1

COMPUTER SALES/WARRANTY
AGREEMENT

175642

<table>
<tr><td rowspan="5">P
R
I
N
T</td><td>NAME OF PERSON OR BUSINESS</td><td colspan="3">STORE NO.</td></tr>
<tr><td>STREET ADDRESS</td><td colspan="3">STREET ADDRESS</td></tr>
<tr><td>CITY   STATE   ZIP</td><td>CITY</td><td>STATE</td><td>ZIP</td></tr>
<tr><td>( )
AREA CODE   TELEPHONE NUMBER</td><td>( )
AREA CODE</td><td colspan="2">TELEPHONE NUMBER</td></tr>
</table>

Effective this_____ day of_____, 19_____, in accordance with the following terms and conditions, you as customer agree to either buy the computer system, software license, hardware, or equipment as listed below from _____, or to lease the same from a third party lessor and _____ agrees to either sell you such equipment or convey the same to a third party lessor for lease to you.

QTY.	DESCRIPTION	STOCK NO.	SERIAL NO.	DATE DELIVERED	PRICE EACH	AMOUNT
					TAX	
					TOTAL	$

CUSTOMER ACKNOWLEDGES BY ITS SIGNATURE THAT IT HAS READ BOTH SIDES OF THIS AGREEMENT, UNDERSTANDS IT AND THAT IT CONSTITUTES THE ENTIRE AGREEMENT, UNDERSTANDING AND REPRESENTATIONS, EXPRESS OR IMPLIED, BETWEEN THE CUSTOMER AND _____ WITH RESPECT TO THE COMPUTER PRODUCTS TO BE FURNISHED HEREUNDER AND THAT NO STATEMENT, AGREEMENT OR UNDERSTANDING NOT CONTAINED HEREIN WILL BE ENFORCED OR RECOGNIZED. THIS AGREEMENT MAY BE ACCEPTED, MODIFIED OR AMENDED ONLY BY A WRITTEN INSTRUMENT SIGNED BY DULY AUTHORIZED REPRESENTATIVE OF CUSTOMER AND A DULY AUTHORIZED OFFICIAL OF _____ OR A SUPERVISOR OF THE STORE MANAGER.

THIS AGREEMENT FURTHER INCLUDES OTHER TERMS AND CONDITIONS APPEARING ON THE REVERSE SIDE HEREOF, INCLUDING _____ WARRANTIES AND LIMITATIONS OF LIABILITY.

ACCEPTED:

BY_____
SIGNATURE

_____
CUSTOMER

_____
PRINT NAME

BY_____
AUTHORIZED SIGNATURE

COPIES 1,2 & 3: Mail to: Manager
      Computer Service Contract Division

_____
TITLE

Fourth Copy: Customer Copy

FIGURE 3-1 *(cont.)*

<u>TERMS AND CONDITIONS</u>

I.   CUSTOMER OBLIGATIONS

    A. CUSTOMER assumes full responsibility that the computer hardware, the equipment and/or software license described on the reverse side meets the specifications, capacity, capabilities, versatility, and other requirements desired by CUSTOMER.

    B. CUSTOMER assumes full responsibility for the overall effectiveness and efficiency of the operating environment in which the Equipment is to function and full responsibility for its installation.

II.   LIMITED WARRANTIES

    A. If the transaction covered by this agreement is a sale and customer is not satisfied with the Equipment, at customer's option, _____ will re-fund the entire purchase price at any time during the thirty (30) calendar day period following the date of delivery of the Equipment; provided the Equipment is returned in new, salable condition (reasonable wear and tear excepted) along with the sales ticket, original packaging, and all manuals. If the applicable transaction is a lease this offer is void and customer's return privileges are governed by the provisions of the lease agreement covering the Equipment.

    B. For a period of ninety (90) calender days from the date of delivery, _____ warrants to CUSTOMER that the Equipment and the cassettes and/or diskettes containing software programs described on the reverse side shall be free from defects. This warranty is voided on items sold or transferred by CUSTOMER to a Third Party. The warranty is void if the unit's case or cabinet has been opened, or if the unit has been subjected to improper or abnormal use. If a defect occurs during the warranty period, the defective product must be returned to a _____ store, franchisee, or dealer for repair along with a copy of the Sales Ticket or Lease Agreement. Except as provided in Paragraph II (A), CUSTOMER'S sole and exclusive remedy in the event of a defect is limited to the correction of the defect by adjustment, repair, replacement, or complete refund, at _____ 'S election and sole expense.

    C. _____ has no obligation to replace or repair expendable items.

    _____ makes no warranty as to the design, capability, capacity, or suitability for use of its Equipment or computer software programs described on the reverse side. Software is licensed on an "AS IS" basis without warranty. CUSTOMER'S exclusive remedy, in the event of a software defect is its repair or replacement within thirty (30) calendar days of the date of purchase upon return to a _____ store, franchisee, or dealer.

    D. Any statements made by _____ and its employees, including but not limited to, statements regarding capacity, suitability for use, or performance of Equipment or software shall not be deemed a warranty or representation by _____ for any purpose, nor give rise to any liability or obligation of _____

    E. Except as provided herein, _____ <u>EXPRESSLY EXCLUDES ALL WARRANTIES, EXPRESSED OR IMPLIED, INCLUDING WARRANTIES OF MERCHANTABILITY AND FITNESS FOR A PARTICULAR PURPOSE.</u>

III.   LIMITATION OF LIABILITY

    A. _____ SHALL HAVE NO LIABILITY OR RESPONSIBILITY TO CUSTOMER OR ANY OTHER PERSON OR ENTITY WITH RESPECT TO ANY LIABILITY, LOSS OR DAMAGE CAUSED OR ALLEGED TO BE CAUSED DIRECTLY OR INDIRECTLY BY COMPUTER EQUIPMENT OR PROGRAMS SOLD, LEASED, LICENSED, OR FURNISHED BY _____., INCLUDING, BUT NOT LIMITED TO, ANY INTERRUPTION OF SERVICE, LOSS OF BUSINESS OR ANTICIPATORY PROFITS OR CONSEQUENTIAL DAMAGES RESULTING FROM THE USE OR OPERATION OF THE EQUIPMENT OR LICENSED SOFTWARE. IN NO EVENT SHALL _____ BE LIABLE FOR LOSS OF PROFITS, OR ANY INDIRECT, SPECIAL, OR CONSEQUENTIAL DAMAGES ARISING OUT OF ANY BREACH OF THIS AGREEMENT OR IN ANY MANNER ARISING OUT OF OR CONNECTED WITH THE SALE, LEASE, USE OR ANTICIPATED USE OF THE EQUIPMENT OR SOFTWARE.

    B. _____ shall not be liable for any damages caused by delay in delivering or furnishing any product referred to in this AGREEMENT.

    C. _____ shall not assume any responsibility for the overall effectiveness and efficiency of the operating environment in which the equipment and software are to function.

    D. No action arising out of any claimed breach of this AGREEMENT or transactions under this AGREEMENT may be brought more than two (2) years after the cause of action has accrued or more than four (4) years after the date of delivery of the Equipment or software, whichever first occurs.

    E. Notwithstanding the limitations and warranties provided in this agreement, _____ 'S liability hereunder for damages incurred by Customer or others shall not exceed the amount paid by Customer for the particular equipment or software involved.

IV.   SOFTWARE LICENSE

    A. _____ grants to CUSTOMER a personal, non-exclusive paid-up <u>license</u> to use the computer software program(s) described on the reverse side hereof. Title to the medium on which the software is recorded (cassette and/or diskette) is transferred to CUSTOMER but not title to the software.

    B. In consideration for this license, CUSTOMER hereby agrees not to reproduce copies of such software program(s) except to produce the number of copies required for personal use by CUSTOMER, and to include _____ 'S copyright on all copies of program(s) reproduced in whole or in part.

    C. CUSTOMER may resell _____ System and Applications Software (modified or not, in whole or in part) described on the reverse side to a Third Party, provided CUSTOMER has purchased one (1) copy of the software for each one resold. The provisions of the software license under Paragraphs IV (A), (B) and (C), for the software sold by CUSTOMER, shall also be applicable to Third Parties purchasing such software.

V.   APPLICABILITY OF AGREEMENT

    A. The terms and conditions of this AGREEMENT are applicable to the transaction described on the reverse side hereof and to all transactions between CUSTOMER and _____ involving computer hardware and software occuring after the signing of this AGREEMENT.

    B. The terms and conditions of this AGREEMENT are applicable to either a sale of the equipment and software license listed on the reverse side hereof to CUSTOMER or to a transaction whereby _____ sells or conveys such equipment to a Third Party for lease to CUSTOMER.

    C. The limitations of liability and warranty disclaimers in this agreement shall inure to the benefit of _____ , the owner and/or licensor of software, and any manufacturer of hardware sold or software licensed by _____ entire agreement, understanding and representations between the customer and ACME COMPUTER COMPANY and that no statement, agreement, or understanding not contained herein will be enforced or recognized. This agreement further includes other terms and conditions appearing *on the reverse side* hereof.

The italicized clause can be very important because of the sales slips certain microcomputer dealers have. One national dealer has a two-sided sales agreement. On the front is an integration clause similar to the one we have given as an example. On the reverse side are 18 paragraphs of fine print indicating its lack of liability to you if neither the hardware nor the software works. The company would not sell you its hardware or software unless you sign the form. If you sign it, you are agreeing that the printed terms control your entire understanding. If a similar clause is on your sales slip, make sure any oral agreement reached with the seller is written on the form and initialed by the sales clerk or store manager. (See Figure 3-1 on pages 45 and 46.)

Comments on the General Rules

Part and parcel of the Statute of Frauds and the Parol Evidence rule are two other "rules of law." A contract can be printed, typewritten, or handwritten. A handwritten change or modification placed on a typed or printed sales agreement will supercede anything printed or typed. Anything typed will supercede anything printed on a document.

> *Example 3-17:* The facts are the same as in *Example 3-14* except an additional sentence is written on the sales slip giving a full cash refund if the goods are returned. The handwritten modification will control the "NO CASH REFUNDS" printed on the sales receipt.

Second, you are presumed to have *read, understood, and assented* to any document you sign or to any terms referred to in the sale. This includes the fine print in advertisements and sales contracts. For example, if the acronym "FOB" (Free On Board) appears, then a specific legal definition is meant (this will be discussed in Chapter 4). If you do not understand what a term or paragraph means, ask the seller. If you do not like a term or paragraph, cross it out on all copies; all parties must initial the change.

Product Availability and Delivery

With all sellers, determine if the goods you want are in stock. This is easy to do in the local store. Walk in and ask to see the product. A mail order company is less simple; the person you talk to may say the product is in stock when it isn't. This may not imply dishonestly; it could be a case of one employee's not knowing what another employee has sold. Although most mail order companies fulfill orders quickly and efficiently, they can and will accept orders for goods not in stock but on order. Under the UCC, unless you set a certain time period, the dealer has a reasonable time to accept the offer by shipping.

What Must Be Delivered

Unless expressly stated otherwise prior to sale, a purchase from a merchant implies that the goods are new. They cannot be used, floor models, factory reconditioned, seconds, or factory rejects. It does not matter if the goods have the same warranty as a new item.

> *Example 3-18:* The buyer prepays for a new printer. If the seller cannot deliver a new printer within a reasonable time, he must refund the purchase price. If the seller offers to deliver a floor demo, for example, the buyer does not have to accept it.

The seller must delivery the exact goods contracted for. If the order is not specific, the seller can deliver any goods that fulfill the minimum requirements.

> *Example 3-19:* The buyer orders 20 BASF diskettes. The seller must deliver BASF diskettes. If no brand is specified, then the seller can deliver any brand.

This concept is very important because of the manner in which mail order computer equipment is advertised. Many times advertisements state that the goods will work with a specific brand of microcomputers, but details are not provided. The goods may fulfill the terms of the advertisement, yet not fulfill the buyer's needs.

> *Example 3-20:* You want a third disk drive for your TRS-80 Model III. You use TRSDOS 1.3 as your disk operating system. TRSDOS 1.3 requires a 6ms track to track access to work. If the track access is greater than 6ms, TRSDOS 1.3 will not work. Other TRS-80 operating systems (e.g., LDOS, DOSPLUS, and NEWDOS) can work with slower disk drives (e.g., 8ms to 20ms). Unless the seller knows you use TRSDOS 1.3, he may deliver a disk drive that does not work with TRSDOS 1.3, yet works with an alternative disk operating system.

If the seller tenders the wrong goods, he may violate the provisions of UCC §2-601 (also known as the Perfect Tender Rule). This section states that substantial compliance with a contract does not allow the seller to force a buyer to accept and pay for nonconforming goods (e.g., the seller delivers Verbatim diskettes instead of the BASF ordered). If the seller delivers nonconforming goods, the buyer has three options: (1) reject the entire shipment; (2) accept the entire shipment; or (3) accept any commercial unit or units and reject the rest.

> *Example 3-21:* You order an Acme Daisy Wheel printer with a proportional spacing print wheel. You take the printer home and discover a pica print wheel was delivered instead. You may take the printer as is, reject both the printer and the wheel and get your money back, or reject either the printer or print wheel. (see *Colonial Dodge, Inc.,* vs. Miler 1982, 116 Mich. App. 78, 322 NW2d 549.)

Partial Delivery

The UCC provides that, unless otherwise agreed, all goods ordered should be delivered at one time. This does not compel the seller to make a single delivery. Following the logic of UCC §2-601 as explained above, the seller can make a partial delivery, giving you the option to accept or reject it. If you do not reject the delivered goods within a reasonable time, you have assented to the partial delivery.

> *Example 3-22:* You order a printer and three spare printer ribbons from the seller. He delivers only the ribbons. You may reject or accept the ribbons. If you do nothing and a reasonable period of time passes, you are deemed to have accepted the ribbons even if the printer can never be delivered.

If partial shipments are not wanted, say so when placing an order. You should inform the local computer shop or mail order company that you are unwilling to accept partial delivery and that all or none of the order should be delivered.

Time of Delivery

UCC Delivery Time

Under UCC §2-309, unless a specific time of delivery is arranged at the time of contracting, the seller has a "reasonable" time to deliver the goods. The UCC has no definition of a reasonable time. It could be next week, next month, or next year. Each case has to be decided independently, taking into account the facts of each case and what the parties intended.

Example 3-23: In July, you order salt to melt snow next winter. The merchant does not deliver salt until late January. Since you can still use salt that winter, the time of delivery was reasonable.

Example 3-24: You buy an Acme Widgetizer that you see in the local store and that is in stock. You are entitled to a quicker delivery than if the item had to be modified by the seller prior to delivery or ordered from an out-of-town supplier.

Example 3-25: You order a computer and state that shipment must be immediate. A delay of eight days is not in compliance with the order.

If a specific time is set in the contract, then delivery *should* (as opposed to *must*) be by that date.

Example 3-26: You write on the sales ticket that "Delivery must be by July 1 or order is cancelled."

The UCC urges reasonable commercial activity. If you specifically limit delivery to prior to July 1 and delivery is not until July 3, you may still be required to take delivery. The fact that the goods were not delivered on the date promised may not relieve you of the obligation to take delivery.

The law has a specific five-word magical phrase that will require delivery by the time set in the contract or relieve you of your obligation to take the goods. The phrase is *"Time is of the essence."* This phrase means that the parties intended time to be a vital and essential term of the agreement and that violating the time would be an *absolute* violation of the contract.

Mail Order Delivery Time

The Federal Trade Commission has defined a "reasonable time" as either the time set forth in the advertisement (e.g., four to six weeks delivery) or if no time is stated, 30 days. FTC Regulation, 16 C.F.R. 435, prohibits mail order companies from failing to deliver their products within the time stated in their advertisements. If no time is set, the goods *must* be shipped within 30 days after receipt of a "properly completed sales order." A properly completed sales order is a document that shows where the product is to be shipped and that payment has been made.

If the seller cannot ship within 30 days, then he is required to notify the buyer of the delay. See Figure 3-2 on page 51.

A buyer has two options. If the seller expects to ship within 30 days, he has the right, prior to shipment, to agree to a new shipping date or get a refund. If the buyer does not respond to the seller's inquiry, he is assumed to have assented to the new shipment date.

FIGURE 3-2
This postcard is the type of post card you should get when a mail order
merchandiser notifies you that it will be unable to ship your merchandise
within the time set forth in its offer or in the 30 days required by the FTC.

A seller can ask a buyer to accept more than one delay, but he
must advise the buyer each time of the right to cancel.

If the seller provides a revised shipping date outside of 30 days
or cannot give a definite revised shipping date, the order is deemed to
be *automatically* cancelled unless the buyer expressly consents to ex-
tend his acceptance within the 30-day period. If the buyer does not
consent to the delay, the seller must refund his money at the end of the
30-day period.

If a mail order sale is cancelled, the seller must make a full
refund of all monies paid within seven business days after cancellation.
If payment was made by credit card, the seller must adjust the account
within one billing cycle.

Practical Hint: If a buyer immediately needs a product, he
should inform any seller *in writing* that (1) immediate shipment is
expected or (2) time is of the essence and that delivery must be received
by a certain date or the order is null and void. By doing this you will
not have to wait two months for goods to be restocked. If a local store is

ordering hardware or software for you, you can give the same delivery restriction.

With a mail order, you should also request that (1) a separate invoice showing what has been shipped be mailed the same day the products are delivered to the carrier for shipment and (2) a separate invoice be attached to the outside of the package. By doing this you can discover before you accept or open the package what has and has not been shipped.

What Price to Pay

If you examine a lot of advertisements, you will see the term "Manufacturer's Suggested List Price" followed by the price. This is the price for which all retailers would love to sell their goods. The "Manufacturer's Suggested List Price" is only a *suggestion*. A retailer may charge *any* price he wants for any product he has in stock. His actual selling price is determined by a variety of factors ranging from his rent to the amount of competition he has. There is nothing to prevent you from offering to pay less than he is asking.

> *Example 3-27:* The suggested retail price for an Acme Widgetizer is $200. You can offer $150. If the seller accepts, that is the price you pay.
>
> *Example 3-28:* The best deal I was ever offered for an IBM PC was 25% off list price. In addition, if I paid cash on a Tuesday, I could get double trading stamps, which could be reconverted back into cash (worth an additional 1% of the purchase price). Every store that sold the IBM PC locally was willing to meet the price.

If you want to bargain with a retail store, there is one rule to remember. Don't offer a lesser price to a person who does not have the authority to strike a bargain with you. A sales person is out to protect his or her commission. The more you pay, the more the sales person makes. The owner, on the other hand, wants to move the merchandise and may be willing to make a smaller amount (while still making a profit) in order to move the merchandise.

Hint: If you make a large purchase (e.g., over $100) at a local store, you should be able to save 2 to 5% of the purchase price by paying cash or using a personal check versus paying by credit card (but see Chapter 5, "How to Pay"). This savings occurs because the seller has to pay a commission (ranging from 1.5% and higher) to the credit card company. By paying cash or using a check, the seller saves the percentage.

Warning: Some retailers, primarily mail order, have a surcharge for buying by credit card. This is against federal law. However, enforcement of this law has not been very good. If a retailer makes this additional charge, you should inform him that this is against federal law and as a consequence you will take your business elsewhere.

Where Will You Buy From? Locally Vs. Mail Order

Buying New Equipment

A buyer has three places to buy new hardware and software: a local store, a mail order company, or the manufacturer or publisher. Each choice has its advantages and disadvantages.

The ideal place to buy hardware and software is the local store. You can test hardware and software before purchasing it to make sure it will fulfill your needs. Unfortunately, a local store has three drawbacks:

1. It cannot have everything in stock. One of the unfortunate facts of life is that the moment you walk into a store to buy something, the last one was just sold!

2. It may be more expensive than mail order. Local stores usually charge the suggested manufacturer's list price. A mail order company discounts its prices. This "discount" can be significant.

   Example 4-1: Wordstar for the IBM PC lists at $495. A typical mail order price is $295.

3. The quality of the sales staff varies greatly. For every knowledgeable sales person, there is an idiot whose knowledge is limited to how to turn the computer on.

Mail order's advantage is that it has (or can quickly get) whatever you want in stock at a lower price than the local store or the manufacturer/publisher. Its major drawback is that you cannot test the goods before purchase. This is very important because most companies have a firm rule that software that has been opened cannot be returned; the rule is based on the assumption you have duplicated the software.

The hardware manufacturer or software publisher has one major advantage over the local store and mail order dealer. It can quickly ship a buyer the latest version of the software/hardware and is more willing and able to answer questions regarding the goods after the sale.

> *Example 4-2:* You have just bought a complicated data base program. Who knows more about it? The sales person who sells it along with 30 others, or the author who has spent the past two years perfecting it?

However, if a problem arises with hardware or software manufactured/published by a large company, it may be difficult to find someone who can give a straight answer or knows what is really going on. The larger the corporation, the more it is compartmentalized.

Buying From the Local Store

Ideally, there should be several local sources at which to buy any equipment. If there is only one local source for a specific product, you may find yourself at the source's mercy when it comes to repairs, customer support, and the like, especially after the product line is discontinued.

If there is more than one local supplier, divide your purchases among them. You will then have business relationships with other stores on whom you can fall back in the event the primary store fails to service you properly.

> *Example 4-3:* Once when I needed to get my computer fixed, the store that sold me the main unit said repairs would take a minimum of five days. The second store, which sold me the disk drives, fixed it within 24 hours.

Choosing a Store To Buy From   The more popular the hardware and software, the more dealers there will be. There are five criteria to consider when choosing a local supplier:

1. What is the primary occupation of the supplier? Strange as it may sound, with many of the smaller, lesser known brands, the supplier does not primarily sell microcomputers.

> *Example 4-4:* An engineering firm is the only supplier of a microcomputer brand in St. Louis. The owner said the firm was so impressed with using the computer in its business that they set up a side business selling it. No stock is kept on hand. Think of the support (or lack thereof) a St. Louis buyer would get.

2. Even if microcomputer sales is the primary business, how much stock is kept on hand? If a store cannot make immediate delivery on a standard disk drive or modem, question the store's finances (i.e., the amount of money behind it). You do not want to be left holding the bag with a computer that cannot be repaired because the local supplier went bankrupt.

3. What is the size of the service area compared to the size of the selling space, and what is the number of service technicians to sales staff? If there are 20 sales people and only one service technician, be wary. The odds are that the service technician will always have a large backlog of repairs and cannot quickly repair your unit.

4. Who is the owner and is she present? Many people are jumping on the microcomputer bandwagon, and some will quickly fall off. If the store is owned by an absentee owner as an investment, she may not know what is happening. Deal with people who have a direct financial stake in keeping you happy.

5. How accessible is the store manager? Can you deal directly with her, or must you deal with a salesperson? When the microcomputer field was small, the salespersons were usually knowledgeable about the goods sold. Today, because of the boom in the microcomputer stores, there are many salespersons who know how to sell but do not know a ROM from a RAM. They are parrots who repeat a rehearsed sales pitch; they have no direct experience in operating the hardware or software. Many times, the only knowledgeable person is the store manager. If she is inaccessible before the sale, just think how it will be after the sale.

Warning: Department stores and the like are now selling computers. Just because a store has a prestigious name does not mean it can provide any better service than another store. A store is only as good as its employees.

Buying by Mail Order

Most consumers consider only the *advertised* price when buying by mail order. *This is the wrong approach!* A number of other points must be examined.

All advertisements must be examined in detail. The information contained in the fine print would shock most people. The following advertisements were contained in one issue of *BYTE* magazine:

> "Defective software will be replaced free, but all software returns subject to 15% restocking fee and must be accompanied by RMA [return merchandise authorization] slip."

The seller agrees to replace the software if it does not load properly. The defective original media must be returned and a replacement will be sent out. If the software is returned for any reason (e.g., you ordered the wrong brand that will not load into your computer), the company's prior written permission must be obtained or it will not be accepted. Even with permission, it will cost 15% ($15 per every $100) of the purchase price to return it.

> "Open merchandise not returnable."

This says it all. How can you test the product without opening the package?

> "Prices subject to change."

This means the advertised price is not binding on the seller. This result arises because the ad copy is prepared months before the advertisement actually runs. Most ethical dealers try not to raise their prices during the life of the advertisement, but a favorite scam of some unethical dealers occurs when payment is by credit card; the goods are shipped and billed at the "current, higher price" (not the advertised price). The buyer is told to ship the goods back if the price is too high. Most people, to save the aggravation, just accept the higher price.

Another favorite scam is informing the buyer, after his check has been cashed, that the goods have gone up in price. He is told he must either pay more money or a refund will be sent. Do not expect the refund in the mail the next day. Months may pass before it is sent.

> "Warranty repairs are done in 48 hours or we will send you a new board."

Shipping time to and from the repair center is not mentioned. It takes a minimum of 24 to 48 hours (and sometimes much longer) to transport the board each way to and from the repair center. Instead of being without the board for two days, it becomes five or six days (and longer if a weekend is involved). Furthermore, since no record of the actual delivery time or date is kept, the 48-hour turnaround time can be fudged.

> "Free Shipping" [at the bottom of the page *Prepaid Cash Orders Only]

This is a favorite advertising technique. The advertisement boldly proclaims "FREE SHIPPING." But elsewhere, in much smaller print, the

"Free Shipping" is limited to prepaid cash orders. If the order is paid by credit card, shipping is extra.

"Personal Checks require two weeks clearance."

Find out if immediate shipment is made if the order is paid by personal check. Most dealers wait two or three weeks for the check to clear. If the dealer waits for your check to clear and you need the goods immediately, it might be better to pay by credit card and get immediate shipment. A variation used by many dealers is to accept personal checks if they are guaranteed by a credit card. The dealer takes the credit card and prepares a sales ticket for it. If the check bounces, the dealer then processes the credit card slip.

"Unless prepaid with cash, please add 5% shipping, handling, and insurance (min. $5)."

Always ask if handling, shipping, and insurance are included in the advertised price. If they are not, find out what they will be. Unless the advertisement explicitly states that they are included, you should assume that they are not. On some items, shipping is such a small amount that it is cheaper to pay the shipping charges and purchase price by credit card 30 days later. Be careful when allowing shipping charges to be added to the bill. Some companies will charge the actual cost, some a flat fee, and others a percentage (as high as 15% in some cases). If you do not ask, you will have no one but yourself to blame when exorbitant shipping and handling charges are added to the low price.

"FOB shipping point [e.g., FOB Denver]"

The acronym FOB means "Free On Board." It is defined in UCC §2-319 and means that the seller's *sole legal obligation* is to place the goods in the possession of the carrier. The sale is completed at that instant, and the seller is then entitled to payment. *ALL RISK OF LOSS NOW BE-LONGS TO YOU!* If the carrier damages or loses the goods in shipment and you have not insured the goods, you will have the dubious pleasure of trying to collect your loss from the carrier. If you had insurance, you may have to wait while the insurance company investigates the claim to make sure it is bona fide. You should consider yourself lucky if the claim is paid within 30 days.

"FOB place of delivery" (i.e., FOB your home town) has an entirely different meaning. The seller, at its own risk and expense, must transport the goods to that place and make delivery.

Warning: If the goods being shipped are insured, find out the name of the insurance company and its relationship to the carrier. Many freight carriers self-insure up to a certain dollar limit; this means that no outside insurance is bought. Since a loss means out-of-pocket expense for the carrier, it behooves the carrier to fight the claim or delay payment. If a substantial amount of money is involved, contact your own insurance agent and buy insurance yourself.

> "Jogging Radio with headphones FREE with purchase of $300 or more."

Nothing is free. If a dealer offers a "Free" bonus, realize that the cost of the free item is built into the cost of the other items sold. The buyer still pays for it.

Mail Order Points to Consider.   There is so much competition among vendors that you should get a minimum of three bids from different dealers. A buyer should not pay for any long distance calls. If the seller does not have a WATS line (an 800 number) that allows free incoming telephone calls or if he does not accept collect calls, try someone else. When asking for a quotation, be sure to tell the seller that it must include insurance and shipping to your home. Otherwise, the least expensive quotation can actually cost more when shipping is added.

> *Example 4-5:* It costs more to ship 50 pounds from Texas to Maine than from New York to Maine. The odds are that the item when purchased in bulk cost the same to a discounter in Texas or New York, so shipping cost to you becomes important.

Do not be afraid to tell a vendor what the competition's price is. Be specific and say "Well, ACME Computer Shoppe just quoted me $50 less for the same item." Most dealers will meet, and some will beat, their competitor's price just to make the sale.

The Federal Trade Commission has regulations and rules regarding mail order selling. A detailed discussion is in Chapter 3, "The Law of Sales." Basically, FTC Regulation, 16 C.F.R. 1435 prohibits mail order companies from failing to deliver their products within the time stated in their advertisements. If no time is set, then the goods must be shipped within 30 days after receipt of a "properly completed sales order."

Find out if shipping includes delivery to a home or business. Some carriers require pickup at their terminals; others deliver only to the entrance of an office building. Moving a bulky 65-pound package may not be your idea of fun.

Never buy mail order from a dealer located in your state. The idea behind ordering by mail is to save money. A seller must collect sales tax on in-state sales. There is no sales tax on interstate shipments.

Before buying hardware through the mail, find out if it can be repaired locally. Sooner or later, it will need repairs. It is a rueful awakening to discover that a $200 saving on a disk drive or a computer is not a savings when:

1. Repairs may be available only in a distant city.
2. Shipping a unit to and from the repair center increases the length of time it will be unavailable for use.
3. You have less leverage in complaining about faulty repairs.
4. You may have to pay shipment costs both ways.

It may be cheaper to pay more locally in the beginning to save money in the end. Always ask under what circumstances the goods can be returned. Not all peripherals work with all computers. What works on an IBM PC may not work with an Apple. See Figures 4-1 and 4-2 on pages 61 and 62.

When comparing prices, be sure identical products are compared. Suppose the following list of hardware and accessories is wanted. You call the local Radio Shack Computer Center and a mail order company and compare prices:

	Mail Order $	Local $
1. TRS-80 Model III with 48K and two disk drives	$1695	$2295
2. Radio Shack printer	480	695
GRAND TOTAL	2305	3170

You add up the figures and say to yourself, "I can save $865 by ordering from the mail order company!" It is not that simple!

First, make sure the prices are for identical equipment or software. There may be subtle differences between them. For example, the $2295 Model III represents a 100% Radio Shack factory original microcomputer with a full Radio Shack warranty. The $1695 represents an almost identical Model III but contains non-Radio Shack disk drives and memory with no Radio Shack warranty.

These differences can be very important. Any Radio Shack Computer Center will fix a 100% Radio Shack computer under the Radio Shack warranty; it will not fix the modified computer under warranty. The modified computer will have to be shipped back to the seller for warranty repairs.

> Example 4-6: A buyer bought a used Radio Shack Model III computer. The computer contained 48K memory and two disk drives. The woman thought she had a pure Radio Shack computer. She took it in for a disk drive repair. It was not until the service technician took the cover off that he noticed it was not a pure Radio Shack computer. Because the drive was not Radio Shack's, he could not repair it.

FIGURE 4-1

RONALD CARTER
1404 E. Central
Jackson, MO 63001

July 20, 1982

Customer Service
Consolink Corporation
1840 Industrial Circle
Longmont, CO 80501

Re: SooperSpooler

Dear Sirs:

　　　Reference is made to my telephone conversation with you
today. I am interested in ordering a SooperSpooler to use with my
IBM PC and Qume printer. Before I order, I would like to know if
I can return it for a full refund if I have any trouble getting
it to work. I am not an computer expert and my ability ends at
plugging the cables in.

　　　I look forward to hearing from you.

　　　　　　　Yours truly,

　　　　　　　Ronald Carter

FIGURE 4-2

CONSOLINK®
CORPORATION

1840 Industrial Circle / Longmont, Colorado 80501 / (303) 651-2014 / 1-800-525-6705 / TWX 910-320-0786

July 20, 1982

Mr. Ronald Carter
1404 E. Central
Jackson, MO 63001

Dear Mr. Carter;

Pursuant to our phone conversation of July 20, I have provided below
an explanation of Consolink's Standard Warranty in addition to our
policy on SooperSpooler returns.

Briefly, each one of our products is burned in and tested prior to its
shipment to ensure its being in perfect operating condition when
received by the customer. If, however, there should be some defect
in workmanship or materials the standard warranty will cover the cost
of repair or replacement for a period of one year. At this time all
units are serviced out of our production facility in Colorado. In
the near future, however, we will have established service reps nation-
wide to assist our customers as needed both during the warranty period
and outside its time constraints. (Please be aware that any modification
of the circuitry not done by Consolink will void the warranty.)

In addition to the return policy inherent in our standard warranty on
parts and labor, Consolink allows returns of the SooperSpooler and
will replace the unit or refund your money if upon receipt of the
SooperSpooler the customer finds that it will not work in his specific
application or if the unit was damaged during shipment. We ask to be
notified of the problem in advance of the return and be given a
tentative ship date. Also, a brief letter detailing the problem should
be enclosed with the returned unit and when possible, the unit should
be returned in the original carton since it was designed specifically
to provide maximum safety for this product.

I hope this letter answers any questions you may have about Consolink's
warranties. Should you need further explanation of the information
provided above or on the product itself, please feel free to call me
at (303) 651-2014.

Sincerely,

Lisa Estabrooks

Lisa Estabrooks
Sales Representative

LE/ek

A Consolidated Packaging Group Company

Be careful when ordering nongame software by mail. Many advertisements list very good prices for software, but they do not state that the software has been superceded by a new and better version or that the author is no longer supporting it.

If one product is going to be used with another product, inform the seller when the quotation is requested. For example, some printers come with either a parallel or serial interface. Each variation has a different price. If the seller is asked only for a quote, he may quote the cheapest model and not the one needed.

How to Order

When placing a mail order by telephone, do the following:

1. Make a note of the date and time called along with the name of the person you speak to.
2. Be very particular in describing the goods you want.
3. Inform the seller that delivery is to be "FOB" your home or business address, and include any other terms regarding delivery that you want.

You cannot simply sit back and await delivery. A conversation alone is worth nothing. Send a letter, keeping a copy for yourself, to the mail order company. In it, make reference to the telephone call, the person you spoke to, and the details of the telephone conversation. Repeat that the order is "FOB" your hometown, that delivery must be made by a certain date, and state any other conditions imposed. Now the requirements of the Statute of Frauds and the Parol Evidence Rule have been fulfilled. This letter has another main advantage. It prevents the unethical dealer from shipping additional items (usually "nonreturnable" software) that you deny ordering but that the seller claims you did. See Figure 4-3 on page 64.

What to Look For

When buying new equipment, try and do the following before paying:

1. Hook up the equipment to make sure it powers up. If a local store says that there is an extra charge for assembling the equipment (i.e., putting boards in, not assembling raw kits), walk away. With competition as it is, another store will assemble it in order to make the sale. Have the equipment assembled in your presence and watch how it is done. You want to learn the correct way of installing boards so you do not later install a 128K RAM board backward and blow it out. For the same reason, boot up the software and make sure it loads.

FIGURE 4-3

RONALD CARTER
1404 E. Central
Jackson, MO 63001

July 23, 1983

The Disk Shop
1901 Byte Drive
Los Angele, CA 91711

Attn: Bill

Re: My order

Dear Bill:

Reference is made to our telephone conversation of this date. I ordered the following from you; (1) a double sided, 40 track Tandon disk drive (with all necessary cables) that will work with my IBM PC; and (2) Wordstar for the IBM PC.

It is my understanding that the goods are in stock and will be shipped immediately. If the goods are not in stock, cancel my order. Do not ship the disk drive without the cable as I cannot use it. Also if I do not receive delivery by August 5th, I will not accept them.

The disk drive cost $400 and Wordstar, $300. This price includes delivery and insurance. The goods are to ship "FOB" my address.

You are authorized to charge my VISA Card, account # 4332-1234-8765, for $700.

If you have any questions, please feel free to contact me.

Yours truly,

Ronald Carter

2. Check the general condition of the shipping container. Was the box brought to you factory sealed or retaped? Some stores take all newly received equipment and run it for 72 hours, hoping that any equipment failures will occur then. Others do not. Regardless, it should not have been resealed more than once or twice. Check to see if there are any big gouges in it. Are there numerous shipping labels on it? Each of these conditions indicates where the shipping box has been. There is nothing that compels you to accept any particular unit or box. If you do not like the looks of one, demand another. It is your right to do so.

3. Inspect the general condition of the unit and supporting materials. Are there any scratches on the unit? (A new unit should have almost none.) Has anyone written in the owner's manual? (This is a very good hint that the equipment has been used.) Compare the serial number on the unit itself to the serial number on the box or warranty card. (If they do *not* match, *do not* take the unit.) If no warranty card is enclosed, find out before you take the unit whether one is normally enclosed (if *any* doubt, contact the manufacturer/publisher).

4. Do not buy complex software without a warranty or registration card!

5. If there is a built-in self-test feature, run it a few times (once is not enough!).

6. If you receive a mail order package that is visibly damaged, do *NOT* accept or open it. Write "REFUSED DUE TO BOX DAMAGE" on the outside of the box or on the receipt. Let the delivery person take it back.

7. If the goods will need cables, make sure they are enclosed. This will save you a return trip to get them.

Buying Used Equipment

There are only two compelling reasons to buy used hardware or software:

1. To save money.
2. To buy equipment no longer manufactured or available new.

   Example 4-7: A Radio Shack Model I Microcomputer Expansion Interface is no longer manufactured or available from Radio Shack.

There are three primary sources for used equipment and software:

1. Individuals (such as members of your local users' group or people who advertise in a local newspaper).

2. A local microcomputer vender who takes equipment in on trade (usually in order to sell new equipment).
3. National microcomputer want ad newspapers such as the *Computer Shopper*.

Rules for Buying Used Hardware and Software

1. *Know what you want and need.* The first-time user should not buy used hardware. He may think he knows what he needs or wants, but he does not. The variety of peripherals and additions for each brand of microcomputers is rapidly growing. Unless he is very confident and knowledgeable, there is an unreasonable risk that he will be "ripped off" (see *Example 4-6*). He should buy and learn with a cheap game computer bought new. This way he will have someone to fall back on when he has his first set of problems. He must learn how to float before he can swim.

If you are confident about what you are doing, write a list of criteria that the hardware or software must fulfill. For example, do you need RS-232 communications? Do you want single or double sided disk drives? Do you need a serial or parallel printer port (or both)?

2. *Find out exactly what is being offered.* Is any software included in the transaction? How recent is it? Has the hardware been user-modified? Who did any repairs? What is the approximate age of the components? The answers to each of these questions not only help determine the value of the equipment but may save you from wasting your money on buying something you do not want or need.

Hint: If the seller does not know the age of the goods, tell him to inspect the serial number. Near the number there may be a plate stating the date of manufacture. If there is no such plate, get the serial number and call the manufacturer, who should be able to state the approximate date of manufacturer on the basis of the serial number.

3. *Find out whether it will really do what you want it to.* This is a lot easier said than done. Because of the number of units and modifications on the market, it is very easy to buy used equipment that will not fulfill your needs.

> *Example 4-8:* You plan to buy a used Radio Shack Daisy Wheel II. You are going to use it to print in a 15-character-per-inch mode. Depending on the age of the printer, it may or may not work. Radio Shack replaced a ROM chip in the Daisy Wheel II. The new chip will work at 15 cpi; the old ROM chip cannot.

4. *What price to pay.* Before knowing what is a fair price for used equipment, find out the manufacturer's suggested retail price and

what the discount mail order's price was. Unless the equipment cannot be bought new (see Example 4-7), it should sell at a maximum of 30% to 40% below the lowest new price.

> Example 4-9: The Radio Shack Daisy Wheel II printer is listed in Radio Shack's Computer Catalogue #9 for $1995. You can buy it new from a mail order house for $1450 (including shipping to your home). Assuming a 30% discount from the lowest current retail price from a discounter, $1015 should be the maximum price for the used printer.

If you are not careful, you can pay more for a used unit than you would new.

> Example 4-10: In an October, 1982, weekend edition of the St. Louis Post Dispatch, a used Osborne Computer was offered for $1695. Its new price at a local computer store was $1795. The same weekend, a mail order discounter, advertising in The New York Times, asked $1595.

5. *How will the goods be delivered?* It is one thing to ship a floppy disk and book through the mail; it is quite another to ship a 130-pound computer across country.

6. *Making the call.* Never just mail money across town or across the country; call and discover if the goods are still available. At that time pull out your list and make sure the goods fulfill your needs. Take notes of what was said. During the call, get the seller's day and night telephone number and his street mailing address. *Do not accept a post office box number.* After the call, contact telephone information in the seller's town. Ask the operator to give you the telephone number on the basis of the name and address you have. If the operator cannot, be wary!

If a price is agreed on, try to get a commitment that the goods have been sold to you. Some sellers will agree to this, and some say the goods are sold to the first person who pays for them.

Hint: If necessary, for approximately $10, you can have a confirming letter and partial payment at the seller's door the next day by using the post office's Express Mail Service, Federal Express, or other similar delivery services.

7. *How to Pay.* Buying used equipment through the mail can be dangerous. Although most people are honest, there is always the rotten apple who wants to steal your money. What better way to steal than to have 20 or 30 people send the same person a cashier's check for the same piece of equipment?

Compounding this risk is that a nonmerchant seller (i.e., a private individual) will demand your money before the goods are shipped.

He does not want to take the risk that you will not pay after you get delivery. If the seller is a merchant, pay by a credit card.

If the seller demands cash up front, suggest the following alternative: Pay the freight and COD charges in advance. The carrier can be instructed to accept cash or certified check only. When the goods are delivered, pay for them and immediately open the shipping container. If the delivery was not what you paid for, notify the carrier of the possible fraud. The carrier will normally retain the money while it investigates. This will not work with postal money orders.

What to Look For In Used Hardware or Software

Apply the same principles used for purchasing new equipment, but be aware of the following additional points.

1. Do not buy used hardware without having diagnostic software. For example, Radio Shack's disk operating system for the TRS-80 Model I and Model III came with a memory tester. There are diagnostic programs available for every major brand of microcomputer, that can do a stress test on disk drives and RAM (some can even test to make sure a disk written on one drive is properly read on another drive).

2. Try to get a provision in the sales agreement that the purchase of hardware is subject to the equipment being inspected by a third party.

3. Never buy used software without first learning the current version number. Saving $100 on a $200 program is not a savings if it costs $100 to upgrade to the current version.

4. Find out if the author or distributor supports a second purchaser. Some support only the original purchaser (they keep a list that correlate the serial number to the buyer). Some software is so complicated that it will be unusable if you cannot get "hand-holding" from the author.

Warning on Buying Used Equipment

When buying used hardware from individuals, you take the risk that you may not receive good title to it. Article 9 of the UCC deals with Secured Transactions. Secured Transactions is how a lender protects its loan to a consumer. Assume that you want to buy a $10,000 computer but do not have the money to pay for it. A lender loans you the money but wants to have some protection. He can get a security interest in the computer. This security interest is very similar to a lien on an automobile. No one can seize the computer from you to pay a debt, without the lender's permission. If the loan is not paid, the lender can seize the computer from you.

The UCC requires the lender to secure its interest by filing a notice. The type of filing required depends on the state. Theoretically, the filing gives notice to the entire world of the lien. Even if a buyer did not know of it, it binds and controls him. If you buy a used computer in the ordinary course of business [defined by UCC §1-201 (9)] from a "person in the business of selling goods of that type" (i.e., a merchant), then UCC §9-307 says you take the computer free and clear from any security interest field. But if you do not buy from a merchant "in the ordinary course of business" and the lender files the appropriate papers with the appropriate agency, then you buy the computer subject to any previously filed security interests. You could pay for the computer, and the lender can legally seize it from you. You would either have to pay off the secured creditor and sue the person who sold it or let the secured creditor take the goods back and still sue the seller for the amount of money paid.

5

How to Pay

Because nothing in life is free, the buyer of microcomputer goods has to pay for his or her purchases. Local buyers usually pay for their purchases by cash, negotiable instrument (check, money order, etc.), or credit card. Additionally, mail order buyers can often arrange payment by interbank wiring of funds or cash on delivery (also known as COD). Each method has its advantages and disadvantages.

Cash

Even though cash is a universally accepted medium of payment, it has many dangers and should rarely be used. Unless circumstances dictate otherwise (e.g., if you can save money by paying cash), do not use it. If you use cash, use it only for small purchases from a local store. Unbelievable as it sounds, law books are full of cases in which people have lost their money merely in the few steps from one bank teller to another.

Never send cash through the mail! If it is lost or stolen in transit, it is solely your loss!

Negotiable Instruments

A negotiable instrument is a piece of paper signed by the *maker* (i.e., the person making the instrument) that contains the maker's unconditional promise to pay a certain sum of money on demand or at a definite time. If you write a check (which is a negotiable instrument), you are the *maker*. Being negotiable, the instrument can be transferred from one person or entity to another; it can be issued to a local store, which endorses it to its landlord to pay the rent, who in turn endorses it to the bank to pay the mortgage. The bank in turn endorses it to another bank to pay off its debts, and so on, *ad infinitum* until it returns to the maker.

Negotiable instruments include such documents as checks and money orders (but not postal money orders).

Checks

Three kinds of checks are used by consumers: personal, certified, and cashiers checks.

Personal Checks.   Most people are familiar with personal checks. Personal checks contain the maker's personal order to his or her bank to pay a certain sum to the maker or to another entity. If a check is presented for payment with a forged endorsement, it can be protested and the maker will not be charged for it.

Certified Checks.   A certified check is a personal check that bears the bank's *signed* agreement that the check will be paid. The bank is promising that the maker's signature is genuine, that the maker had the authority to write the check, and that there is sufficient money in the maker's account to honor the check.

A check may be certified by either the *drawer* (i.e., the maker, who is person making the check) or the payee (i.e., the person to whom the check is made payable). A bank does not certify a check until it determines that there are or will be sufficient funds to pay the check when it is presented for payment. A bank either debits the account immediately or puts a "hold" on it. When a hold occurs the amount certified cannot be withdrawn from the account until the check is paid. This difference is very important. If the checking account pays interest, the amount certified will collect interest until the check is presented for payment. If it is debited immediately, interest collection stops.

Hint: Whenever a check is certified, make sure the check's magnetic ink coding is obliterated. Otherwise, the check may "accidentally" be paid twice because the bank's computer cannot read the certification. If the magnetic code is present, the check can be processed without human intervention. If it is obliterated, the computer rejects the check, and a bank clerk will manually process it.

Cashier's Checks.   A cashier's check is a certified check drawn on the bank itself. The bank, and not the drawer (maker), is making the promise to pay the check. On issuance of a cashier's check, the bank immediately debits the drawer's account and credits its own account.

Certified vs. Cashier's Check: Practically speaking there is no difference between a certified check and a cashier's check. The only time it makes a difference is when the bank does not immediately debit the drawer's account on a certified check but instead "holds" the money. In this case, it is more advantageous to use certified checks.

Stopping Payment on Checks

Personal Checks.   The issuer of a personal check can always stop payment on it by so instructing the bank. An oral stop payment is effective for only 14 days whereas a written stop payment order is effective for six months. Any check more than six months old is considered "stale," and a bank has no obligation to accept it.

When you give a stop payment order, it is *very important* that you list five items as the subjects of the letter and that you write them accurately, *especially* the amount. See the sample letter in Figure 5-1 on page 73. Notice that it gives the account number, the check number, the date the check was issued, the payee's name, and the amount of the check. The bank takes the stop payment order and instructs its computer to flag any check the amount of which equals the amount set forth in the order. The rejected check is then examined taking into account the other information given.

If the wrong amount is given, e.g., $450.98 instead of $450.48, the bank may pay the check and be relieved of liability because of your error.

A stop payment order must be received in time to allow the bank a *reasonable* opportunity to act.

> *Example 5-1:* On the morning of July 14, the bank is instructed in writing to stop payment on a check. The check is presented for payment that day. The bank may not have received sufficient time to act. Compare this to when the check is presented for payment on July 29. Then sufficient time has been given.

If a check is paid after the bank receives a valid stop payment order, UCC §4-403 (1) and (3) provide that an actual loss must still be proven in order to recover damages from the bank. Even if a loss is suffered, the bank is liable for only the lesser amount—the amount of the check or the amount of the loss.

FIGURE 5-1

RONALD CARTER
1404 E. Central
Jackson, MO 63001

November 1, 1983

Customer Service
Second American Bank of St. Louis
111 Olive Blvd.
Clayton, MO 63105

Re: Checking account #: 657-357-12
       Check #: 297
       Date Issued: October 31, 1983
       Payee: Gee Whiz Computer Company
       Amount of Check: $456.54

Dear Sirs:

    You are hereby instructed to stop payment on the above described check that was drawn on my checking account #657-357-12.

    If there is a charge for this service, you are authorized to automatically debit my account.

    Please send me written confirmation acknowledging that you received this letter.

          Yours truly,

          Ronald Carter

Example 5-2: You pay for a $1000 computer by check. You go home and decide you do not want it. You make no effort to return it. Even though you instruct the bank to stop payment in sufficient time, it pays the check. You sue your bank. You are entitled to nothing because you did not suffer a loss.

Example 5-3: The circumstances are the same as in Example 5-2, but the computer was already damaged when the box was opened and the seller refuses to repair or replace it. In its damaged condition it is worth $600. Because you have a $600 item your loss is only $400. You can recover $400.

Certified and Cashier's Checks.   Payment *cannot* be stopped on a certified or cashier's check unless fraud or some other illegality is present.

Example 5-4: A printer is ordered COD from an out-of-town supplier. The delivery company is paid with a cashier's check. The box is opened, and two gallon bottles filled with water are found inside. The buyer can stop payment provided the check has not already been paid.

It is not always possible to stop payment on a cashier's check or a certified check. Banks do not like to stop payment on them. The bank can (and often does) require the drawer (maker) to "indemnify" the bank (i.e., agree to pay all expenses) if the bank incurs any expenses or suffers any loss because of the check. Furthermore, some states prohibit stop payment orders on certified or cashier's checks unless you claim that the check was lost.

Example 5-5: A check is made payable to the Acme Computer Company. It is lost or misplaced, and Sam Jones, a thief, finds and cashes it. Because only Acme was *supposed* to cash it, the person who took it from Sam Jones will have to recover from Jones, or make compensation out of his own pocket.

If you allege that the check was lost or misplaced, the bank may allow you to stop payment provided it issues another check to the same person. If you ask the bank to recredit your account or otherwise return the money to you without your returning the check, the bank will probably require you to indemnify it against loss.

Money Orders

There are three distinct types of money orders, and each operates differently. Money orders can be issued by banks, money order companies, and the United States postal service. Money orders are usually used by people who do not have personal checking accounts. They provide an inexpensive, safe, and readily acceptable way of transferring funds.

Bank Money Orders

As the name implies, bank money orders are money orders issued by banks. They are similar to cashier's checks and are usually signed by a bank officer. The bank charges an issuing fee (usually $1 to $2), but if you have an account in the bank, ask for the fee to be waived. Do not confuse a bank money order with a personal money order sold by a bank.

Personal Money Orders

Personal money orders are not issued in a bank's name or by the postal service. Depending on your state's regulation, the money order company can range from a large company such as the American Express Company to a small mom-and-pop operation. Personal money orders are very similar in nature to personal checks.

A personal money order can easily be bought at a wide variety of business establishments such as a drug store, grocery store, gas station, and the like. The seller fills in only the amount; the rest is blank and must be filled in by the purchaser.

Do not keep the money order blank. If it is lost, a finder could fill in his name and cash it. Although you can stop payment on a lost personal money order, whoever accepts it may suffer a financial loss.

Warning: Personal money orders can (and have) become worthless the moment after they were bought. A personal money order is only as good as the company issuing it. No protection exists for companies that issue personal money orders regardless of whether they are big national companies or minuscule operations. The United States government stands behind its postal money orders. Banking is a highly regulated industry, and many times a year independent auditors examine a bank's books. If a bank fails, there are procedures to protect the account holders.

Stopping Payment on Bank and Personal Money Orders.   The rules for stopping payment on a bank money order is the same as for cashier's checks. Only if fraud is alleged or the money order is lost will the bank stop payment.

Although payment on a personal money order can be stopped, it is easier said than done. The company that issued it must be given sufficient notice, which entails filling out a form and paying a fee.

Miscellaneous Points about Bank and Personal Money Orders. If a bank or personal money order is lost in the mail, the purchaser may have to wait a minimum period of time before a replacement or refund is issued. The bank or money order company wants to make sure the money order is really lost and not just delayed.

Furthermore, it can be difficult and time-consuming to discover if a personal money order has been cashed.

> *Example 5-6:* You send the Fly By Night mail order company a money order to pay for software. It says it never received payment. With a check or bank money order, the bank can quickly determine if it has been cashed. With a personal money order, forms must be filled out and processed.

Postal Money Orders

Postal money orders are issued by the United States Postal Service. The rules concerning them differ sharply from the rules for bank or personal money orders. The postal money order system exists "to furnish the public a safe and cheap method of transferring small sums of money. The government carries on the system, not for gain, but to supply a public need . . ." *Bolognesi* vs. *United States*, 2nd Cir. 1911, 189 Fed. 335.

The rules and regulations concerning postal money orders are stated in §941 of the *Post Office Domestic Manual.* Every post office has this manual available for public inspection.

Postal money orders are sold only by the United States Postal Service. Depending on the size of the order, the service charge ranges from $0.75 to $1.55. The maximum amount per postal money order is $500. To buy $600 in a postal money order, two money orders must be issued and two service charges collected.

A postal money order can be paid for either by cash or by "established" travelers' checks. If paid by travelers' checks, the postal money order issued must be at least 50% of the value of the travelers' checks; this prevents the Post Office from being used as a bank.

Once the postal money order is issued, the buyer must fill in his name and address and the name and address of the payee on the postal money order and receipt. If both are not completed, the Postal Service does not guarantee a 100% refund if a claim is made.

Unlike a personal money order, if the purchaser loses a blank postal money order, no replacement or refund will be issued. It is a complete loss for the purchaser. Likewise, if the receipt is lost, no refund will be issued.

By law, postal money orders are not negotiable. They cannot be passed from person to person to settle debts, like a personal check. If someone offers you a postal money order made payable to another person or business, do *not* accept it. Under federal law a postal money order that has been endorsed more than once (e.g., it was not deposited directly in the payee's bank or taken to the post office to be cashed) is null and void.

Lost, Damaged, or Improperly Endorsed Postal Money Orders. Only the owner or payee can replace or inquire about the status of a postal money order by filling out a form. A minimum of 30 days must pass before a postal money order can be replaced. You must fill out and complete Postal Form 6401. Notice that the illustration on p. 78 states that 60 days must pass before a replacement can be issued. All current forms are out of date. The *Postal Manual* states that 30 days must pass.

Form 6401 may be obtained at any Post Office or by writing to:

Money Order Division
Postal Data Center
Post Office Box 14695
St. Louis, MO 63182

A photocopy of a paid money order can be ordered by completing Postal Service Form 6065. See Figure 5-3 on page 79. This form is available at your local post office or by writing to:

Money Order Division
P.O. Box 14965
St. Louis, MO 63182

A request for a photocopy can be filled only within two years of payment. After that, the postal money order is destroyed.

Stopping Payment on a Postal Money Order. Payment on a postal money order cannot be stopped. It is good for 20 years! If there has been a forgery or improper payment (i.e., if someone has forged the payee's signature or otherwise altered the postal money order), then both you and the payee must complete a Claim/Questionnaire Form 1510 (see Figure 5-4 on page 81). If you think that a postal money order has been lost in the mail, then the same form must be completed and processed.

FIGURE 5-2

NO WAITING PERIOD FOR FILING INQUIRIES. REPLACEMENT MONEY ORDERS MAY NOT BE ISSUED UNTIL 60 DAYS AFTER THE ORIGINAL DATE OF ISSUE.

MONEY ORDER SERIAL NO.	AMOUNT OF ORDER		ISSUE DATE		
	DOLLARS	CENTS	YEAR	MONTH	DAY

CAUTION—Applicant should verify this data for correctness

NAME OF ISSUING POST-OFFICE AND ZIP CODE (NOT STA. OR BR.) *(Print)*

NAME OF PURCHASER *(Print)*

NAME OF PAYEE AS WRITTEN ON MONEY ORDER *(Print)*

IF NOT PAID, ISSUE A DUPLICATE MONEY ORDER TO:
NAME *(Print)*

STREET ADDRESS *(Print)*

POST OFFICE, STATE AND ZIP CODE *(Print)*

HAVE YOU REQUESTED A REPLACEMENT
FOR THIS MONEY ORDER BEFORE ☐ YES ☐ NO

I CERTIFY THE INFORMATION ON THIS FORM IS TRUE AND AGREE TO REPAY THE POSTAL SERVICE, UPON DEMAND, THE AMOUNT OF THE REPLACEMENT MONEY ORDER IF THE ORIGINAL IS ENDORSED BY THE DESIGNATED PAYEE-

SIGNATURE

WARNING: The making of any false or fraudulent claim against the United States or statement in support thereof is punishable by fine or imprisonment or both.

If a photocopy is requested then fee must be paid. Photocopy available for TWO (2) years from date of payment.

DO NOT USE THIS FORM FOR AN INQUIRY OR TO GET A PHOTOCOPY OF AN INTERNATIONAL MONEY ORDER.

FOR POSTAL BUSINESS ONLY

INFORMATION ONLY - DO NOT ISSUE RE-PLACEMENT MONEY ORDER *(Check if applicable)* ☐

POSTMASTER OR FRB: *(Check if photocopy required)* ☐

PHOTOCOPY FEE ONLY

AFFIX 30¢ STAMP HERE AND CANCEL

PS Form 6401, Apr. 1979

DOMESTIC MONEY ORDER INQUIRY

FIGURE 5-4

NOTE

1. This form should only be used for ordinary and certified mail, insured parcels from Canada, and registered mail exchanged with Canada. Use Form 3812, Request for Payment of Domestic Postal Insurance, to report loss or rifling of COD and domestic insured mail. Use Form 565, Registered Mail Inquiry for Delivery and/or Application for Indemnity, to report loss or rifling of domestic registered mail.

2. Be sure all applicable items in Part II are completed.

3. For any questions relating to this form, see Section 255 of the Postal Operations Manual.

(REMOVE THIS PORTION BEFORE MAILING)

PART I

Postal Customer:

The sender of the article described below has made an inquiry regarding delivery of the item. The article was not located at the mailing office; therefore, we are contacting you to determine if the article has been delivered. Please indicate below if the article has been received, and return the form in the enclosed PREADDRESSED ENVELOPE WHICH REQUIRES NO POSTAGE. Your response will assist the Postal Service in providing improved service. **PLEASE RETURN BOTH PARTS I AND II-A.**

THANK YOU

THE ARTICLE WAS	DATE OF REPLY	SIGNATURE OF ADDRESSEE OR AGENT
☐ RECEIVED *(Date if known)* _____ ☐ NOT RECEIVED ☐ REFUSED		

REMARKS

PS Form 1510, Feb. 1980

PART II-A

U.S. POSTAL SERVICE

MAIL LOSS/RIFLING REPORT

1. COMPLAINT DATE	2. OFFICE ACCEPTING COMPLAINT *(City and State)*	3. COMPLAINT ☐ LOSS ☐ RIFLING

4. ARTICLE WAS MAILED BY	5. ARTICLE WAS ADDRESSED TO
A. NAME	A. NAME
B. RETURN ADDRESS AS ON ARTICLE MAILED	B. ADDRESS ON ARTICLE
C. CITY D. STATE E. ZIP CODE	C. CITY D. STATE E. ZIP CODE
F. DAY TELEPHONE NUMBER *(Include Area Code)*	F. DAY TELEPHONE NUMBER *(Include Area Code)*

6. ARTICLE MAILED			7. ARTICLE WAS SENT	8. TYPE OF MAIL
A. DATE MONTH DAY YEAR	B. HOUR ☐ AM ☐ PM		☐ 1ST-CLASS ☐ PARCEL POST ☐ OTHER *(Specify)*	☐ LETTER ☐ PARCEL ☐ OTHER *(Specify)*

9A. SPECIAL SERVICES	9B. CANADIAN MAIL ONLY
☐ SPECIAL HANDLING ☐ SPECIAL DELIVERY ☐ CERTIFIED NO.	☐ INSURED NO. ☐ REGISTERED NO.

10. PLACE OF MAILING	NAME AND/OR ADDRESS OF LOCATION CHECKED	
☐ MAIN POST OFFICE ☐ STATION OR BRANCH ☐ COLLECTION BOX ☐ RESIDENCE OR BUSINESS	CITY AND STATE	ZIP CODE FOR LOCATION CHECKED

11. CONTENTS OF ARTICLE *(Describe in detail, size, color, brand name, serial no., check no., and amount, etc.)*	12. VALUE $

PS Form 1510, Feb. 1980

In COD sales, as with FOB shipments, the buyer owns the goods the moment they are placed in the hands of the carrier. The seller retains only a lien on the goods and has the right of possession until they are paid for.

The amount of a COD charge should not dissuade anyone from ordering COD. In fact, ordering COD can save money.

> *Example 5-7:* You order a $1000 printer and pay by cashier's check. Assuming 5.5% interest, the monthly income on the $1000 would be $4.58. As of March, 1983, United Parcel Service's COD charge was $1.50. Unless the package is received within 10 days from the date the cashier's check was purchased, you lose more in unearned interest than in the COD charge.

Before ordering COD, ask the seller how it delivers COD purchases. The post office requires payment by money order. If you do not have sufficient cash on hand to buy the money order when the postman first attempts delivery, you may have to go to the post office. The United Parcel Service will accept a personal check, a certified, or a cashier's check, depending on the seller's instructions.

Credit Cards

Nearly every dealer, whether mail order or local, accepts credit cards as payment. The procedure is simple: The buyer gives the seller his credit card or its number. The seller verifies that the card is not stolen and that the amount of the purchase is not above the store's limit. If it is above the limit, the seller calls the credit card company and get its approval for the purchase. If approval is granted, the buyer gets the merchandise; if it is denied, the seller will so inform the buyer.

Credit cards are controlled by the Fair Credit Billing Act [15 U.S.C. §§1666 through 1666(j)]. They are the safest form of payment. If a card is lost or stolen, the holder is liable for only the first $50 of unauthorized charges made by someone else. The liability will be less if the credit card company is informed of the loss before any charges are made.

A seller is not allowed to impose a surcharge for credit card purchases [see 15 U.S.C. §1666f(a)(2)]. Nevertheless, some companies are charging for their use. Before paying by credit card, verify that the price quoted includes payment by credit card.

Credit cards companies are required to send card holders periodic notices on how to resolve billing problems. The notices read approximately as follows:

FIGURE 5-5

RONALD CARTER
1404 E. Central
Jackson, MO 63001

December 15, 1983

Customer Service
VISA Credit Card
POB 8777A
Fort Lauderdale, FL 33337

Re: Ronald Carter
      Account #: 4332-1234-8765
      Reference #: 8345514
      Seller's Name: The Disk Shop; 1901 Byte Avenue; Los
          Angeles, CA
      Amount in Dispute: $700.00

Dear Sirs:

      Please be advised that I want to protest the above charge.
The Disk Shop sent me the wrong merchandise and it was returned
to them on May 19, 1983.

      Please credit my account. If you have any questions, please
feel free to contact me.

                        Yours truly,

                        Ronald Carter

cc: The Disk House

In Case of Errors or Inquiries About Your Bill

Send your inquiry in writing on a separate sheet so that the creditor receives it within 60 days after the bill was mailed to you. Your written inquiry must include:

1. Your name and account number (if any).
2. A description of the error and why (to the extent you can explain) you believe it is an error.
3. The dollar amount of the suspected error.

If you have a problem with property or services purchased with a credit card, you have the right not to pay the remaining amount due on them if you first try in good faith to return them or give the merchant a chance to correct the problem. There are two limitations on this right:

1. You must have bought the property or services in your home state, or if not within your home state, within 100 miles of your current mailing address.
2. The purchase price must have been more than $50.

National credit card companies such as VISA, Master Card, or American Express rarely enforce the restrictions regarding purchase location and the minimum $50 requirement. If the buyer lives in Maine and orders something from Hawaii, he may still protest the charge and get the credit card company's help in resolving the problems that arise.

Finally, a buyer does not have to pay until the goods are received.

Example 5-8: On March 29 a product is ordered and paid for by credit card. On April 25 the credit card bill arrives showing the purchase but the goods have not yet arrived. The bill can be protested and not paid.

Put it in Writing

Some credit card companies allow a card holder to telephone about their problems. This is not advisable. Always put the complaint in writing. If an acknowledgement is not received within 30 days, send another letter. *Do not put the letter in with the payment.* It should go to the separate address mentioned in the bill. See the sample letter on page 83.

General Comment

Red Flag Warning

If a merchant seller requires advance payment by money order, cashier's check, or certified check, ask why. Offer to put down a small deposit with the balance to be COD. Although there may be a good reason for the seller's requirement, it does not look good. Find out how long the seller has been in business, if he can give you any references, and so on. When buying from a merchant, *never* make the check or money order payable to an individual. Make it payable only to the company name.

Fundamental Differences Among Forms of Payment

The fundamental difference among credit card, COD, and any other form of payment is one of possession and control. If you prepay an order, the seller will already have the money. If he violates any of the restrictions previously placed on the sale (or if he does not even ship the goods), you have to get your money back. If payment is by credit card or COD, you retain the money, and the seller has to get it from you. Whenever you have the choice between paying by credit card or COD, pay by credit card because the credit card has built into it a way of resolving customer disputes.

The Law of Warranties

It is an unfortunate fact of life that products break down or do not work as expected. Consumers assume that their protection lies in the manufacturers' warranties. Nothing could be further from the truth. Written warranties exist for only two purposes:

1. To limit a manufacturer's liability in the event the goods are defective. tive.

    Example 6-1: A defective $2 diskette can do more than $2 worth of damage. Think of the cost to reenter a week's worth of data lost because of media failure.

2. To help market the goods.

    Example 6-2: In 1960 Chrysler had 14% of the new car market. By 1962 its share had dropped to 9.6%. In 1963 Chrysler started a five-year or 50,000-mile warranty. Sales increased more than 30% in 1963, and by 1968 Chrysler had 16.2% of the market.

This chapter deals with warranties: what they are, the applicable law, how warranties are disclaimed, and what cannot be disclaimed.

Warranties are mentioned in the Bible. In the Middle Ages, product quality was overseen by the craftsmen's guides. In the fourteenth century, the manufacturer of faulty merchandise could go to jail for injuring the local town's reputation. In the seventeenth century, merchants developed the system of establishing standards, and quit dealing with merchants who did not meet those standards. This system is still used today.

Until this century, an individual consumer was able, under the doctrine of freedom of contract, to agree to any terms he or she wanted to with the seller. Because most consumers did not know what they were agreeing to, unscrupulous sellers took advantage of them, and the doctrine of *caveat emptor* (buyer beware) grew to be the law.

At all times, both past and present, the law has said that a consumer could negotiate and bargain with the seller or manufacturer about warranties. *This is simply not true.* I have been unable to find any reported cases in which an individual was able to negotiate or bargain a better warranty prior to the sale than that ordinarily given by the manufacturer of the mass-produced consumer item.

When a consumer buys a product, he or she rarely inquires about the warranty terms. The sales person might say there is a 90-day or one-year warranty, but the details are not examined. The typical consumer's first knowledge of the specific warranty terms comes from a piece of paper marked "WARRANTY" that is in the box with the item. This paper typically states that the item is "free from defects in materials or workmanship." See page 88 for a typical warranty.

> *Example 6-3:* One camera warranty stated that the camera was "built with the highest standards and should provide you with years of satisfaction." Two paragraphs later the company limited its warranty to 90 days.

The typical warranty then states that the company will "replace the item if it proves defective with either a new or *reconditioned* unit" or will attempt to repair it "using new or *reconditioned* parts." Notice the word *reconditioned.* It means that even though a new item was bought and paid for, the buyer may still get a used or somewhat less valuable item after the repair.

Finally, there will be a clause in the warranty that reads approximately as follows:

> This warranty is the only warranty available on this item, and is made expressly in lieu of all other warranties including any implied warranty of merchantability or fitness for a particular purpose.

Until 1975, the basic law concerning express and implied warranties could be found only in the UCC. The law was the same for a small consumer purchase or a large industrial transaction. The UCC warranty provision contained provisions dealing with the creation of express and implied warranties, the disclaimer of warranties, and the limitation of remedies if the warranty was broken. In 1975, the United States Congress passed the Magnuson–Moss Warranty Act—Federal Trade

FIGURE 6-1

LIMITED WARRANTY

For a period of 90 days from the date of delivery, _____
warrants to the original purchaser that the computer hardware
unit shall be free from manufacturing defects. This warranty
is only applicable to the original purchaser who purchased the
unit from _____ company-owned retail outlets or duly
authorized_____ franchisees and dealers. This warranty
is voided if the unit is sold or transferred to a third party.
This warranty shall be void if this unit's case or cabinet is
opened, if the unit has been subjected to improper or abnormal
use, or if the unit is altered or modified. If a defect occurs
during the warranty period, the unit must be returned to a
_____store, franchisee, or dealer for repair, along
with the sales ticket or lease agreement. Purchaser's sole and
exclusive remedy in the event of defect is limited to the
correction of the defect by adjustment, repair, replacement,
or complete refund at_____'s election and sole expense.
_____ shall have no obligation to replace or repair expen-
dable items.

Any statements made by_____ and its employees,
including but not limited to, statements regarding capacity,
suitability for use, or performance of the unit shall <u>not</u>
be deemed a warranty or representation by _____ for any
purpose, nor give rise to any liability or obligation of
_____.

EXCEPT AS SPECIFICALLY PROVIDED IN THIS WARRANTY OR IN THE
_____ COMPUTER SALES AGREEMENT, THERE ARE NO OTHER
WARRANTIES, EXPRESS OR IMPLIED, INCLUDING BUT NOT LIMITED
TO ANY IMPLIED WARRANTIES OF MERCHANTABILITY OR FITNESS FOR
A PARTICULAR PURPOSE. IN NO EVENT SHALL _____BE
LIABLE FOR LOSS OF PROFITS OR BENEFITS, INDIRECT, SPECIAL,
CONSEQUENTIAL, OR OTHER SIMILAR DAMAGES ARISING OUT OF ANY
BREACH OF THIS WARRANTY OR OTHERWISE.

Commission Act. This law applies only to consumer products, not large commercial transactions between business. Magnuson–Moss significantly altered the pre-1975 law by setting minimum standards for warranties.

Uniform Commercial Code

Under the UCC, there are two types of warranties: express and implied. Express warranties can arise only by the deliberate actions of the parties to the sale. Implied warranties are created by statute and become part of every transaction unless disclaimed by the circumstances or by the seller prior to the sale.

Express Warranties

Express warranties are defined in UCC §2-313(1). They can be created in three ways:

1. Any affirmation of fact or promise made by the seller to the buyer that relates to the goods and becomes part of the bargain creates the expressed warranty that the product shall conform to the affirmation or promise.

   Example 6-4: A manufacturer says its computer will operate the CP/M operating system.

This express warranty can be created either orally or by a writing (but do not forget the requirements of the Parol Evidence Rule discussed in Chapter 3). It can be a seller's voluntary statement or an answer to a specific question. It can be contained in an advertisement, a sales brochure, a product label, and the like.

2. Any description of the goods that is made part of the bargain creates the expressed warranty that the goods shall conform to the description.

   Example 6-5: A buyer orders a disk drive because the advertisement for it says that it can hold 360K of data. If it cannot, the expressed warranty is violated.

3. Any sample or model that is made part of the basis of the bargain creates the express warranty that the whole of the goods shall conform to the sample or model.

   Example 6-6: A buyer wants to buy 1,000 diskettes. The seller gives him 10 diskettes to sample. On the basis of the sample, the buyer orders the other 990. However, the 990 are not of the same quality as the first 10. The expressed warranty is broken.

A sample is more specific than a model; therefore, the finished product must more closely resemble a sample than it resembles a model.

Warning: The seller will try to limit his or her liability for express warranties. If the seller or a salesperson makes an express warranty that is important to you, write it down on the sales ticket and get it initialed by the seller. Otherwise, the Parol Evidence Rule may prohibit you from introducing any evidence of the oral agreement. Another point to consider is the "lack of authority" clauses found in many sales agreements. An example is the following:

> This agreement may be modified or amended only by a written document duly signed by an authorized official of the company or a store manager.

This clause means that the salesperson can promise you the moon, but the promise is not binding on the vendor or the manufacturer. If there is an important addition to the contract and you are using the seller's form, besides having the salesperson initial or sign the addition, have the sales manager or owner initial the modification. If he or she is not present, you should not sign the form until he or she returns and initials the change.

Puffing.   Puffing arises when the seller makes an affirmation of the value of the goods or gives his opinion or commendation of the goods [see UCC §2-313(2)].

> *Example 6-7:* The seller says, "This is an A-1 quality used computer," or "This program is reliable and user-friendly."

The seller is not creating an express warranty with these statements. You can no more grasp them than you can grasp a puff of smoke. The more specific a statement is, the more likely it is to be deemed an express warranty.

> *Example 6-8:* The circumstances are the same as in *Example 6-7*, but the seller further states that the used computer "will not need major repairs." *Cf. Cagney* vs. *Cohn*, D.C. Super. 1973, 13 UCCRS 998.

Basis of the Bargain.   The UCC requires before an affirmation of fact, description, or model/sample can become an express warranty, it must go to the *basis of the bargain*. This phrase is not defined *per se* in the UCC. However, in the UCC's official comments, a statement is made that particular reliance on a seller's statement does not need to be proved or shown for it to be made part of the deal. As a practical matter, any statement made to a buyer by a seller becomes part of the basis of the bargain unless a clear contrary intention is shown.

Implied Warranties

Implied warranties are created by the UCC and are a part of every sale unless properly disclaimed. The UCC creates two types of implied warranties: fitness for a particular purpose and mechantability. For either type of implied warranty to arise, the seller must be a merchant with respect to the goods of the kind sold. UCC §2-104(1) defines a merchant as "a person who deals in goods of the kind or otherwise by his occupation holds himself out as having knowledge or skill peculiar to the practices or goods involved in the transaction."

There is seldom any question of whother or not a seller is a merchant when the seller is a manufacturer, wholesaler, or retailer of the goods in question.

> *Example 6-9:* A used microcomputer is bought from the local new car dealer.
> *Example 6-10:* A used microcomputer is bought from a neighbor who is a plumber.
> *Example 6-11:* A new microcomputer is bought from a department store.

In Examples 6-9 and 6-10 no warranty arises because the car dealer and neighbor do not ordinarily sell microcomputers. In Example 6-11, the warranty arises because the department store typically sells a wide variety of goods, including microcomputers. It is a merchant even if less than 0.001% of its sales are computer-related.

Merchantability (UCC §2-314).   Merchantability means that the goods offered for sale are of the general kind described and are reasonably fit for the ordinary purposes for which they were intended.

> *Example 6-12:* A car without an engine is not merchantable.
> *Example 6-13:* A disk drive that catches fire on the first day of ownership is not merchantable.

The concept of merchantability is that all consumers have certain assumptions about the products they buy. One assumption is that the product will work with regularity. The fact that the item may violate an express warranty does not mean that it is unmerchantable.

> *Example 6-14:* The fact that an automobile only gets five miles to the gallon instead of the 30 advertised does not mean it is unmerchantable.

Fitness for a Particular Purpose (UCC §2-315).   When the seller at the time of contracting has reason to know a particular purpose for which the goods are required and that the buyer is relying on the seller's skill or judgment to select or furnish suitable goods, the concept of fitness for purpose becomes part of the transaction.

> *Example 6-15:* A buyer tells a seller that he needs a modem that works at 300 and 900 baud. The seller recommends a modem that works only at 300 baud.

For the implied warranty of fitness for particular purpose to be part of the deal, the buyer must actually rely on a seller's skill or judgment. If he tells the seller he wants a specific brand, he is not relying on the seller's skill, and there is no implied warranty of fitness for a particular purpose. This warranty is rarely applicable against the manufacturer of consumer goods because the manufacturer rarely recommends any specific product to a consumer. It is usually an independent agent, such as a retail store, that makes the recommendation.

The implied warranty of fitness for a particular purpose can provide a buyer with his most effective safeguards. It is very difficult for a seller to deny knowledge if he participated in the installation of the system by recommending equipment, performing design work, or furnishing software.

Disclaimers

Many sellers find it advantageous to prepare sales contracts and agreements that limit or disclaim their warranty liability to the buyer. An example is the following:

> EXCEPT AS SPECIFICALLY PROVIDED IN THIS WARRANTY OR IN THE ACME COMPUTER COMPANY SALES AGREEMENT, THERE ARE NO OTHER WARRANTIES, EXPRESSED OR IMPLIED, INCLUDING BUT NOT LIMITED TO ANY IMPLIED WARRANTIES OF MERCHANTABILITY OR FITNESS FOR A PARTICULAR PURPOSE.

A disclaimer can sharply limit your protection against loss. UCC §2-316(2) permits disclaimers of warranties, as follows:

> (2) Subject to subsection (3) to exclude or modify the implied warranty of merchantability or any part of it the language must mention merchantability and in case of a writing be conspicuous, and to exclude or modify any implied warranty of fitness the exclusion must be by a writing and conspicuous. Language to exclude all implied warranties of fitness is sufficient if it states, for example, that "There are no warranties which extend beyond the face hereof."

Another way to disclaim the warranties is to state that the goods are sold "AS IS" or "WITH ALL FAULTS." Because very few people would buy new merchandise sold "AS IS" or "WITH ALL FAULTS," these words are seldom used.

Merchantability. To validly disclaim warranty of merchantability (UCC §2-314), the disclaimer must specifically mention the word "merchantability" or state that the goods are sold "AS IS" or "WITH ALL FAULTS." The UCC implies that it is possible to disclaim merchantability orally. However, this is rarely done. If merchantability is disclaimed in a writing, then the writing must be conspicuous. Any other type of disclaimer is sure to fail.

Fitness for a Particular Purpose. To validly disclaim warranty of fitness for a particular purpose (UCC §2-315), the disclaimer must be conspicuous and in writing. Another way to disclaim it is to state specifically that there is no warranty of particular purpose. Unless the disclaimer is so written, the implied warranty is *not* disclaimed and remains in force.

Conspicuousness. The requirement of conspicuous is difficult to determine. There are numerous court cases holding in specific instances what is and is not conspicuous. The UCC defines "conspicuous" in §1-201(10), as follows:

> (10) "Conspicuous": A term or clause is conspicuous when it is so written that a reasonable person against whom it is to operate ought to have noticed. A printed heading in capitals (as: NON-NEGOTIABLE BILL OF LADING) is conspicuous. Language in the body of a form is "conspicuous" if it is in a larger or other contrasting type or color. But in a telegram any stated term is "conspicuous." Whether a term or clause is "conspicuous" or not is for decision by the court.

If a disclaimer appears in capital letters in a contrasting type face to the other printed faces surrounding it and the disclaimer on the whole is in larger type than the rest of the agreement, it is conspicuous. A conspicuous disclaimer will draw your attention to it. If it does not draw your attention, it is not conspicuous. It does not matter if the disclaimer is on the last page of a 10-page sales agreement. If it is conspicuous, it will fulfill the requirements of the UCC and be upheld. If it is indistinguishable from the rest of the sales agreement, it fails to be conspicuous.

Some sellers are sneaky and will put their disclaimer under some other heading such as "Guarantee" or "Warranty." The warranty provisions are listed, followed by a conspicuous disclaimer. Any seller who does this is taking a risk. This approach is not liked by the law, and a court may disallow a disclaimer placed under a warranty heading. *Cf. Dorman* vs. *International Harvester Co.*, 1975, 46 Cal. App. 3d 11, 120 Cal. Rptr. 516.

Timing of the Disclaimer

Prior Knowledge

Did the buyer know of the disclaimer prior to the purchase? The UCC does not require actual notice or knowledge of the disclaimer. As previously stated in Chapter 3, a buyer is presumed to have read, understood, and assented to any document he signed. If the disclaimer fulfills the requirements of the UCC and the buyer did not see it, he is nevertheless presumed to have read and agreed to it.

There are some instances in which the disclaimer is not printed on the sales ticket or sales contract, nor is it otherwise prominently displayed. The seller, nevertheless, claims the buyer knew or should have known of the disclaimer. Such an argument fails in court. *Cf. Wilson* vs. *Marquette Electronics, Inc.*, 8th Cir. 1980, 630 F.2d 575.

A warranty cannot be disclaimed after a sale is made or after the agreement between the buyer and seller is reached. A warranty disclaimer first presented in the owner's manual or in other material delivered after the sale is void and not worth the paper it is printed on. *Zoss* vs. *Royal Chevrolet*, Ind. Super, 1972, 11 UCCRS 527, and *Dorman* vs. *International Harvester Co., ante.*

Warning: "Warranty Registration" cards are enclosed in most consumer goods. These cards state that the purchaser should mail the card back for "registration." Except for a highly limited situation under the Magnuson–Moss Warranty Act, you do not have to mail the card back. To enforce the warranty, all you need is proof of the date of purchase. If you return such a card (for example, to get a back-up copy of protected software), then cross out all the unacceptable terms (at a minimum those saying you accept the terms of the warranty) and make a photocopy of the edited version.

Disclaimer by Examination.   UCC §2-316(3)(b) states that if a specific item is examined before purchase, then any defects that *should have been* discovered are disclaimed.

> *Example 6-16:* A buyer buys a green CRT, but an orange CRT is delivered.

The test of what you should have discovered is subjective. A microcomputer repair person will be held to a higher standard of examination than will a history teacher.

Warning: The disclaimer by examination also applies if the buyer refuses to examine the goods being sold. The salesperson does not come out and state, "You must examine these goods prior to sale," but he or she might say, "Please examine the computer before taking it home, so there won't be any problems." A refusal to examine the goods for whatever reason brings into effect the disclaimer by examination. If the same or similar words are said to you, be on your guard.

State Limitation on Warranty Disclaimers

Some states have modified the UCC's provisions regarding disclaimers.

In Kansas, the Kan. Stat. Ann. §50-639 (1976) provides that a supplier may not exclude, modify, or otherwise attempt to limit the implied warranties of merchantability and fitness for a particular purpose except to those particular defects that the seller acknowledges before the sale. In the case of a controversy between a consumer and a merchant, the supplier must prove "that the consumer had knowledge of the defect or defects." Furthermore, if a consumer wins a lawsuit based on a breach of warranty, the court may also order the supplier to pay the consumer's attorney's fees.

In Maine, the Me. Rev. Stat. Ann., Title 11, §2-316(5) (Supp. 1982) states that warranty disclaimers shall not apply to the sale of consumer goods or services. Any language, either written or oral, used by a seller or manufacturer, that attempts to exclude or limit any implied warranty or modify any remedy for breach of the warranty shall be void.

In Maryland, the Md. Com. Law Code Ann. §2-316.1 (Supp. 1982) states (1) that the seller (as opposed to the manufacturer) may not disclaim the implied warranties, but (2) that if the seller is held liable it may recover any damages from the manufacturer.

The statute further provides that the manufacturer may not limit a buyer's remedies to recover for breach of warranty unless the manufacturer provides "reasonable and expeditious means of performing the warranty obligations." Thus, if it takes an unreasonable period of time to "perform the warranty obligation," the warrantor (which can be the seller in some circumstances) can be liable for damages in addition to repairing or replacing the item.

In Massachusetts, the Mass. Gen. Laws Ann., Ch. 106, §2-316 (Lawyer's Co-Op, 1976) says that any attempt by a seller or manufacturer to limit its implied warranties on the sale of consumer goods or services shall be unenforceable in the state. Any attempt by a manufacturer of consumer goods to limit or modify a consumer's remedies for a breach of express warranties is unenforceable unless the manufacturer maintains facilities within Massachusetts to provide "reasonable and expeditious performance of [consumer] warranty obligations." Thus a manufacturer can limit its express warranty liability by maintaining or supporting repair facilities within the state.

In Michigan, the Mich. Stat. Ann. §19.2313(2) (1981) states that if a product is broken while still under a warranty for more than 10 days or 10% of the warranty period, then the warranty period shall be extended for the number of days the goods are being repaired.

If the goods are to be repaired at your home or place of business, then the time period shall also include the date from which the buyer notifies the merchant or warrantor *in writing* (a telephone call is not sufficient) that the goods are inoperative. This can be particularly important if repair parts must be ordered.

In Minnesota, the Minn. Stat. Ann. §325G.19 (1981) states that the seller cannot disclaim the implied warranty of merchantability or fitness for a particular purpose.

In addition, subsection 3 of the statute provides that if a manufacturer (1) makes an express warranty and (2) authorizes a retailer to make repairs or perform services under the terms of the expressed warranty, the manufacturer shall be financially liable to the retail seller for an amount equal to what the retail seller would have charged you had your repair not been under the warranty. This helps the consumer in that if the retail seller must absorb part of the cost of warranty repairs, the retail seller may not be as willing or inclined to make the best repairs possible.

In Mississippi, the state has never passed UCC §2-316, and thus there is no provision under Mississippi law to disclaim implied warranties. This means that warranty disclaimers are totally ineffective in Mississippi. Furthermore, in Miss. Code Ann. 1972, §75-2-719(4) (1981), which deals with a buyer's remedies in the event of a breach of warranty, there is the statement that any attempted warranty limitation depriving a buyer of a remedy to which he may be entitled for the breach of the implied warranties of merchantability or fitness for a particular purpose is strictly prohibited.

In New Jersey, the N.J. Rev. Stat. §56-2-1 (1981) has limitations on how warranty time periods are computed. For any consumer product that costs less than $1000 and that is warranted for 90 days or less, the day the warranty begins shall be the day the consumer product is received or installed. The termination date shall exclude any period of time the entire product or any part thereof is in the possession or control of the seller or his agent for repair or otherwise.

In Vermont, the Vt. Stat. Ann. Title 9A, §2-316(5) (Supp. 1982) states that for "new or unused consumer goods or services, a seller or manufacturer may not disclaim or modify any implied warranty of merchantability or fitness for a particular purpose."

In Washington, the Wash. Rev. Code §62A-316(4) (Supp. 1982) provides that for personal, family, or household goods, no blanket disclaimer of merchantability or fitness for a particular purpose will be allowed. If a seller wants to disclaim these implied warranties, he must "set forth with particularity the [exact] quality and characteristics which are not being warranted."

In West Virginia, the W. Va. Code §46A-6-107(1) (1980) flatly prohibits any exclusion, modification, or limitation of any express or implied warranties in a consumer transaction.

In California, the *Song–Beverly Consumer Warranty Act* (Civil Code §1790, ff) is the most extensive state consumer warranty law. It liberally defines "consumer goods" as any machine, appliance, or like product that is used or bought primarily for personal, family, or household use.

The statute urges every manufacturer of consumer goods sold in California with express warranties to maintain in the state sufficient service and repair facilities to carry out the terms of its warranties. In the event it does not maintain "sufficient facilities," then it shall be liable to every retail seller of such manufacturer's consumer goods. The liability shall be determined in one of three ways:

1. In the event of replacement, an amount equal to the actual cost to the retailer, the cost of transporting the goods plus a reasonable handling charge.
2. In the event of service and repair, an amount equal to that which would be received by the retail seller for like services rendered to retail customers who are not entitled to warranty protection, including actual and reasonable cost of the service and repair, cost of transporting the goods plus a reasonable profit.
3. In the event the seller is unable to replace the goods and must reimburse the purchase price, the amount actually reimbursed, plus a reasonable handling charge.

If a consumer suffers a personal injury or financial loss, and if the court or jury decides that the manufacturer willfully violated the terms of the California statute, then the consumer may receive triple damages (i.e., three times the actual loss). A retail seller is also entitled to triple damages and reasonable attorney fees if a manufacturer willfully violates the statute.

Advertising Warranties

A seller cannot disclaim any express warranties made in its advertising material. If an advertisement says a product will do something, then that *particular point cannot be disclaimed:*

> *Example 6-17:* Radio Shack's TRS–80 Microcomputer Catalogue RSC–9 states that the SuperScripsit word processing program can "save and recall multiple paragraphs . . . align tabs, automatic pagination, . . . [It] supports underline, double underline, boldface, super and subscript, and multiple column printing . . ." Yet the warranty that comes with the program says the program is sold "on an as is basis without warranty."

The disclaimer is invalid as to the specific advertising claims because the law feels that a buyer should be able to rely on specific advertising claims.

Failure of Essential Purposes

A disclaimer will not excuse failure to supply the "goods" forming the basis of the bargain. The goods can be merchantable and fit for the particular purpose but still not good for the application wanted by the consumer.

> *Example 6-18:* A communication software package must be able to communicate. If it cannot accurately unload or download information, it fails its essential purpose. The seller did not deliver what was bargained for.

If the goods bargained for are not supplied, the contract has not been fulfilled, and the buyer is entitled to a refund of the purchase price on the theory that the seller never made delivery.

Limitation of Remedies

Under UCC §§2–718 and 2–719, a seller may limit a buyer's remedies in the case the seller breaches one of the express or implied warranties. For example:

> In no event shall the Acme Computer Company be liable for loss of profits or benefits, indirect, special, consequential, or other similar damages arising out of any breach of any express or implied warranty or otherwise.

This provision does not bother most buyers because their broken or defective goods are quickly repaired or replaced under the terms of the express warranty. Another example is the following:

> The Acme Computer Company warrants that it will repair or replace any item manufactured by it that is found to be defective within 90 days of purchase.

But this limitation is not foolproof. Under special circumstances, the limitation will be voided by a court:

> Example 6-19: A brand new disk drive catches fire and destroys the entire computer.

If the seller cannot or will not repair or replace the goods, then its promise to repair or replace is broken. The entire warranty may fail in its essential purposes. With the failure of the warranty, the limitation of remedies will fail. The entire gamut of UCC remedies may become available. These remedies may include recovering damages for the actual, consequential, and incidental losses. In addition, if there is fraud, malice, or gross negligence (e.g., if the seller says he has fixed the same specific problem four times in four weeks), then punitive damages may be recoverable.

Magnuson-Moss Warranty Act

According to a series of Presidential Task Force and Federal Trade Commission reports on warranties, consumers have been unhappy with the warranty service they have received. The two most common complaints are the poor quality of warranty service and the refusal of the warrantor or his agent to do the warranty work. One report examined over 200 different warranties for a wide variety of consumer items: televisions, automobiles, and the like. The average warranty length was between 300 and 600 words. Typical requirements included returning the "warranty registration" card as a condition of getting warranty coverage, limiting coverage to the initial buyer, and requiring the buyer to pay shipping costs of items returned for repair. Out of more than 200 warranties, only one did not contain a limitation or disclaimer!

The Magnuson–Moss Warranty Act (hereinafter referred to as the Act), 15 U.S.C. §§2301–2312, was passed in order to solve some of the problems that arose under the Uniform Commercial Code and state law. Congress felt that if it passed a uniform law the consumer would have a better understanding of his or her rights. It was the hope of Congress that the Act would make consumer warranties easier to understand, prevent deceptive practices, and provide an effective means of enforcing warranty obligations.

Definitions

The Act uses unique definitions that must be understood prior to any discussion of it. They are discussed in the next several paragraphs.

A *consumer product* is any tangible personal property normally distributed in commerce and normally used for personal, family, or household use. Such products include automobiles, typewriters, microcomputers, and the like. They do not include an aircraft engine (*Patron Aviation, Inc.* vs. *Teledyne Industries, Inc.*, 1980, 154 Ga. App. 13, 267 SE2d 274). If an ambiguity exists as to whether an item is a consumer product, the ambiguity is resolved in favor of coverage.

> *Example 6-20:* IBM sells a variety of computers. An IBM 360, a mainframe, is not a consumer product under the Act. But the IBM PC, which is sold to consumers (as consumer is defined by the Act), is a consumer product.

Under this definition "canned" computer software (such as Visicalc) would be classified as a consumer product.

A *consumer* is (1) a buyer (other than for purposes of resale) of any consumer product, or (2) any person to whom such product is transferred during the duration of any implied or written warranty (or service contract) applicable to the product, or (3) any person entitled under state law to enforce the obligations of the warranty against the warrantor.

A *supplier* is any person engaged in the business of making a consumer product directly or indirectly available to consumers, and includes people in the chain of production and distribution of a consumer product. It does not include those who do not regularly engage in the business of making consumer products directly available to consumers.

A *warrantor* is any supplier or other person who gives or offers to give a written warranty or who may be obligated under an implied warranty.

The term *other person* includes third parties who promise to refund, replace, or repair. Thus, the *Good Housekeeping* Seal of Approval is covered by the Act.

> *Example 6-21:* "If any product which bears [the Good Housekeeping Seal or which is advertised in this issue of the [Good Housekeeping] magazine . . . proves to be defective at any time within four years from date when it was first sold to a consumer, we, *Good Housekeeping*, will replace the product or refund the purchase price."

The term *other person* does not include a supplier who only supplies or delivers to a consumer the warranty on a consumer product given by another supplier or manufacturer of the product.

> *Example 6-22:* A computer store that only passes to the buyer the manufacturer's warranties covering the goods is not a warrantor.

If the supplier or retailer acts as a warrantor by making repairs, adjustments, and the like without telling the consumer to contact the warrantor, then the supplier or retailer may be deemed to have accepted the manufacturer's warranty and may be sued under it (*Richards* vs. *Goerg Boat & Motors Inc.*, Ind. App. 1979, 384 NE2d 1084).

A *service contract* is a written agreement to perform services, over a fixed period of time, relating to the repair or maintenance (or both) of a consumer product.

A *written warranty* is (1) any written affirmation of fact or written promise made in connection with the sale of a consumer product by a supplier to a buyer that relates to the nature of the material or the quality of workmanship and affirms or promises that such material or workmanship is free from defect or will meet a specified level of performance over a specified period of time; or (2) any undertaking in writing in connection with a sale by a supplier of a consumer product to refund, repair, replace, or take other remedial action with respect to the product in the event the product fails to meet the specifications set forth in the undertaking. There is a fundamental difference between these two definitions and the express warranties of the UCC. If no time period is mentioned, then no warranty is created under the Act.

> *Example 6-23:* Under the UCC, saying tha a disk drive can access a track in 6 ms. will create an expressed warranty; not so under the Act. To create a warranty under the Act, the manufacturer must say that the disk drive can access a track in 6 ms. during a specific time period such as the first year of ownership.

Statements such as "Satisfaction Guaranteed or Your Money Back" do not create express warranties provided the statement is general. If a supplier makes this type of statement about only one item, however, then it is a warranty.

Full Vs. Limited Warranty

The Act does not require that a warranty be provided. Neither the Act nor the Federal Trade Commission can prescribe the warranty duration or any substantive terms for any product.

If a supplier voluntarily provides a warranty and the item costs more than $10.00, the warranty must be designated as either "Full [length of duration] Warranty" or "Limited Warranty."

If any warranty is given, the following information must appear in the warranty:

1. To whom the warranty is extended.
2. A clear description of what is covered by the warranty.
3. A statement of what the warrantor will do under the warranty.
4. The duration of the warranty.
5. The name and mailing address of the warrantor or a toll-free number the consumer can call to get the information.
6. A step-by-step explanation of what the consumer must do to get warranty performance.
7. The following statement: "This warranty gives you specific legal rights, and you may also have other rights which vary from state to state."

Full Warranty.   A full warranty requires that the warrantor remedy the defect within a reasonable time and without charge. If the supplier installed the item, then it must be removed and reinstalled without charge unless it is reasonable to require a consumer to remove and reinstall the unit.

> *Example 6-24:* It would be unreasonable to expect the average consumer to install or remove an internal disk drive in a TRS–80 Model III. It would be reasonable to expect him to unplug the cable from an external disk drive for the same computer.

If the warranty period is for a fixed time (e.g., one year), the warranty coverage must include all consumer owners who own the product during the warranty period. This means that any subsequent owner of an item that is still under a full warranty has the right to use the warranty. However, a warrantor can limit the duration to "as long as you own the product." This means that the first owner will have a full warranty for as long as he or she owns the unit but that the warranty will cease as soon as title to the goods is transferred.

If the unit cannot be fixed after a reasonable number of attempts, the consumer is entitled to a refund of the purchase price or a replacement with either an identical or equivalent new product.

The provider of a full warranty cannot require an unreasonable duty as a condition of receiving warranty service. Unreasonable duties include the following:

1. Requiring the consumer to pay the cost of mailing or shipping the unit back to the warrantor. The warrantor can require the consumer to

prepay these costs provided the consumer is refunded this cost at the end of the repair.
2. Requiring that the unit be returned in its original package.
3. Requiring the consumer to obtain warranty service from the selling or installing dealer when the warrantor has more than one warranty service point.
4. Requiring the consumer to return a warranty registration card.
5. Requiring notice of the defect to be in writing.

Limited Warranty.   Any warranty that is not a full warranty is a limited warranty, and there are three major differences between the two. First, the limited warranty may limit coverage to the first purchaser only (i.e., the warranty is not transferable). Second, the warrantor can require that you return the warranty registration card as a condition of getting the warranty coverage, provided that this requirement is disclosed in the warranty. Third, the warrantor can require you to pay for shipping and for reasonable service charges for the repair.

Magnuson–Moss and Disclaimer of Implied Warranties.   If a warrantor issues a full warranty, he cannot disclaim the implied warranties of fitness for a particular purpose or merchantability that arise under state law (which is the UCC in most cases).
    If the warrantor issues a limited warranty, the duration of the implied warranties may be limited to a reasonable duration provided the limitation is "clearly disclosed" (i.e., conspicuously located) on the face of the warranty [see 15 U.S.C. §2308(b)]. Any attempt by a seller or manufacturer to disclaim the implied warranties altogether violates the Act (see *Ventura* vs. *Ford Motor Company*, 1980, 180 NJ Super. 45, 433 A.2d 801). It is arguable that if a manufacturer violates the Act, then all disclaimer and limitation of remedy provisions are null and void. This means a consumer could also sue for punitive damages.
    If the seller or manufacturer enters into a service contract with the consumer within 90 days of the sale, then the seller or manufacturer cannot disclaim the implied warranties so long as the service contract is in effect.
    Hint: See Chapter 9 on some of the problems of service contracts. If you do buy a service contract, do not be penny wise and pound foolish. The Act severely limits a manufacturer's or a seller's rights to disclaim implied warranties if a service contract is bought from either of them. It may not be worth the savings to buy a cheaper service contract from a third party.

Warranty Tie-Ins.   A warrantor cannot require a tie-in on goods costing more than $5.00. A tie-in is a condition that requires the consumer to use a specific brand to secure or improve a warranty.

> *Example 6-25:* The Acme Disk Drive Company cannot require you to use Acme brand diskettes to keep its disk drive warranty in force.

A tie-in will be allowed if the warrantor can objectively prove to the satisfaction of the Federal Trade Commission that the requirement is reasonable (e.g., if Acme can objectively prove its particular brand of diskettes causes less head wear than any other brand of diskettes on the market).

A warrantor is prohibited from giving better terms if the consumer buys something extra along with the warranted item.

> *Example 6-26:* The Acme Disk Drive Company cannot give a 90-day warranty on its disk drive when it is bought alone and an 180-day warranty when it is bought along with 10 Acme diskettes.

If the warranty provides for only the replacement of defective parts and does not include a labor charge, the warrantor cannot require that the warrantor or its authorized service facilities install the replacement.

Finally, a warrantor cannot require that its authorized repair service do maintenance work to keep the warranty in force. Anyone can do the maintenance work. All the consumer must prove is that the maintenance was done.

Knowledge of the Warranty.   All sellers must have copies of the applicable warranties available for inspection prior to any purchase. Congress made this requirement in the hope that consumers would investigate the warranty coverage and buy the product with the best warranty.

If the seller is a mail order house, it must either print the full text of the warranty in the catalogue or sales solicitation, or it must disclose that the warranty is available free upon request.

Differences Between the UCC and the Act

There are two major differences between the Act and the UCC. They concern attorney's fees and the way an aggrieved party may enforce his or her rights.

Attorneys' Fees

Attorneys' fees can be a major impediment in getting warranty satisfaction. With attorneys' fees starting at $45 an hour on up, only the very rich or the very poor (who are entitled to free legal aid) can afford to litigate warranty claims. The rest of society must just suffer along.

In a UCC law suit, each party has to pay its own legal fees. It is not hard to see that a major corporation with retained attorneys could bankrupt the individual consumer. The Act changes this imbalance of power.

Under 15 U.S.C. §2310(d)(2), a court may, unless it thinks it inappropriate, award attorneys' fees "based on actual time expended" and "reasonably incurred" in the prosecution of the claim. Almost all Act lawsuits examined have allowed successful plaintiffs to recover their attorneys' fees and expenses, so that the middle class is enabled to retain private attorneys to enforce their rights.

> Example 6-27: In Ventura vs. Ford Motor Company, ante, a case dealing with the revocation of acceptance of an automobile, the attorney took the case on a $350 retainer plus whatever the court awarded. The plaintiff won a $7000 verdict, and the court awarded attorneys' fees of $5000.

Enforcement of Rights

Under the UCC, a consumer must prove that the seller made a warranty under the UCC, that the goods failed to live up to the warranty, that the consumer's loss was caused by the defect, and that the consumer suffered damages as a result.

Under the Act, once a warrantor has been given reasonable opportunity and failed to cure a breach of its warranty or service contract, he or she may be sued in either state or federal court. Any person damaged by the failure of a warrantor to comply with his or her obligations under the Act may sue.

Acceptance and Rejection of Goods

A buyer has the duty to accept and pay for any goods contracted for and delivered in accordance with the expressed terms of the sales agreement or the implied terms of the UCC. If any aspect of delivery or tender is not in accordance with those terms, the buyer does not have to accept delivery.

Inspection

UCC §2-513 gives a buyer the unqualified right, except in COD sales, to inspect the goods at any reasonable time and place and in any reasonable manner before accepting them. The inspection can be either before or after the buyer has obtained exclusive control of the goods.

 If the terms of sale require payment before acceptance, payment must be made unless any nonconformity in the goods appears without inspection.

> *Example 7-1:* A Commodore microcomputer is ordered, but an Apple II/e is delivered.

However, UCC §2-512(2) specifically provides that any prepayment does not constitute acceptance of the goods.

 A buyer may take and inspect the goods elsewhere provided the inspection is done within a "reasonable time." If not done within a "reasonable time," the goods are deemed to be accepted. The length of time for inspection can be extended if the seller instructs the buyer to test the goods further.

Example 7-2: A new printer does not work as described in the instruction manual. You write the seller who instructs you to try another method of operation.

Keep a dated record of any conversations with the seller when he tells you to do a further inspection. If the seller sends you a letter, save it.

The goods may be operated in order to inspect it. "Operation" consists of more than just turning a device on and making sure it appears to work.

Example 7-3: A hardware spooler has hardware and software controllable features. The hardware features work, but to test the software-controllable features you must program the unit. You are allowed a reasonable time to do the programming.

Once you determine that the goods are unsuitable and that you will reject them, you may not continue to operate them without risking that the continued operation will be construed as an acceptance.

Any expense incurred in the inspection (e.g., laboratory fees) is the buyer's expense except when the goods do not conform to the sales contract and are rightfully rejected. In such cases the inspection expenses may be recovered from the seller.

Example 7-4: An 80-track dual-sided disk drive is ordered from a mail order company. Upon delivery it does not work properly so it is taken to a local technician, who charges $10 and states that it does not work properly because it is a 40-track single-sided drive. The expense is recoverable from the seller.

The recoverable expense does not include repairs, only the expense of ascertaining whether the goods fulfill the sales agreement.

There is a *qualification* though. Just because the law says the expense is recoverable does not mean you can get it. You can demand that the seller reimburse you, but if he refuses, you will have to file a law suit to enforce your rights. It may not be worth it.

If the goods are not inspected, UCC §2-606(1)(b) states that there is no implied warranty with regard to any "defects which an examination ought in the circumstances to have revealed."

Example 7-5: You inspect and buy a battery, but you fail to notice that it is leaking acid. The leakage is apparent to all. Acceptance may not be later revoked because of the leakage.

You are required only to find defects that are easily discovered. You do not have to find those defects that are not discoverable by a reasonable inspection or are latent. In these cases, you have a reasonable time to find them without breaching the contract.

Example 7-6: You order a "100% factory original Posh home computer with all Posh parts" from El Slezo computer store. Six months later you take the computer into an authorized Posh repair service and are told that El Slezo used Cheapo parts to upgrade the unit. At this point you have not technically accepted the unit.

See Chapter 4 for a detailed discussion of what to look for in an inspection.

Failure to Pass Inspection

As stated earlier in Chapter 3, "The Law of Sales," under the UCC's perfect tender rule, if the goods fail to conform totally to the contract or to the requirements of the UCC, a buyer may do one of the following:

1. Reject the whole.
2. Accept the whole.
3. Accept any commercial units and reject the rest.

Acceptance

The UCC has three tests of what is acceptance, as follows:

Test 1

When the buyer, "after a reasonable opportunity to inspect the goods," informs the seller that the goods are conforming or that he will retain them in spite of nonconformity, the demands of Test 1 are met.

Example 7-7: Before buying it, a buyer tests a $200 computer program for 10 hours at the seller's place of business. By this inspection he is deemed to have accepted the goods. Compare this to the case that would exist if he tested it for only 10 minutes.

Example 7-8: Buyer wants to trade-in his used microcomputer for a newer model at a local store. The retailer examines the computer and says he will accept it in trade. But the next day the retailer refuses to take the computer because he notices that he had missed a defect. He must take the unit because he had an opportunity to inspect it before he said he would accept it.

Example 7-9: A buyer writes or calls the seller immediately after delivery and says he accepts the goods.

Warning: Never state in writing or orally to the seller that you have inspected the goods and that you accept them as is. Be especially on guard whenever a seller demands that you sign a form stating that you have inspected and accepted the merchandise before he allows you to take possession of it. Then and there, do a complete and full inspection of each and every component that makes up the product. In addition, handwrite on the form that the goods are accepted only insofar as they can be inspected under the circumstances and that you have not completed tests to disclose all defects. If this is unacceptable to the seller, walk away from the transaction.

Acceptancy must be voluntary. If you are tricked into accepting a product, it is not a good acceptance. However, the courts are divided on whether or not an acceptance contained in an agreement signed by you (even though you claim you did not know of the acceptance) is valid. Always read what you sign!

Test 2

If the buyer did not within a "reasonable time" reject the goods or notify the seller of the rejection, then Test 2 applies.

> *Example 7-10:* You order five 10-meg hard drives for your factory. On March 1, 10 80-track floppy drives are delivered instead. Your staff allows the equipment to sit more than four months before opening the boxes. You are deemed to have accepted the goods because of the time involved.

Four criteria are used in determining the reasonableness of the inspection time:

1. The difficulty of discovering the defect (i.e., was it blatant or hidden?).
2. The terms of the contract.
3. The relative perishability of the goods (e.g., you have less time to reject apples than steel).
4. The course of action after the sale and before rejection.

Test 3

When the buyer does any act inconsistent with the seller's ownership, such as reselling the goods, modifying them, and so on, Test 3 applies.

> *Example 7-11:* You modify a newly purchased computer by cutting a hole in it. You have accepted the unit regardless of its condition.

Use of the goods does not constitute acceptance by itself. The goods can be "used" for the purpose of inspecting them. Once a reasonable inspection has occurred, however, continued use may be deemed an acceptance.

Once the goods are accepted, a buyer cannot later reject them or revoke his acceptance for any visible defect that should have been reasonably discovered in an inspection.

> *Example 7-12:* You ordered a Posh Computer with the instructions that two Posh disk drives be installed internally. The seller delivers the computer with two clearly marked Cheapo disk drives instead. If you do not reject the computer immediately, you cannot later reject or revoke acceptance because Cheapo disk drives were installed.

If a defect is not discoverable by a reasonable inspection and the buyer does not know of it, he or she is excused from rejecting the goods until the nonconformity is discovered.

> *Example 7-13:* A buyer orders a microcomputer with fast RAM chips. The seller installs slow chips instead. Five months later, the buyer cannot get a program to work. He takes the computer in for servicing and is told that the failure is caused by the slow chips. Because the buyer would have no reason to know or suspect that slow chips were used, any previous inspection was not final.

Rejection

A buyer can reject any goods that do not fulfill the exact requirements of the sales contract, including partial delivery, untimely delivery, and so on. Rejection is the combination of the buyer's refusal to keep non-conforming goods and the notification thereof to the seller. UCC §§2-602 through 2-604 control rejection.

Notification

Upon rejecting goods, a buyer *must* within a reasonable time, notify the seller of his rejection. Failure to notify the seller will cause the rejection to fail. The reason(s) for rejection should be as specific as possible. *Mere notice of poor quality is not sufficient!*

What To Do When Rejecting Goods. Whenever rejecting goods for any reason whatsoever, whether it be the wrong color, delivery one minute after the time called for in the contract, or whatever, the buyer should immediately notify the seller by telephone. This should be done even if it means the buyer must pay for a long distance telephone call. Make a note of the person you speak to and what each of you said. List all known defects, no matter how minor they appear.

FIGURE 7-1

RONALD CARTER
1404 E. Central
Jackson, MO 63001

October 15, 1983

Ms. Henriette Jackson
Customer Service
Mail Order Division
The Disk Shop
1901 Byte Drive
Los Angeles, CA 91711

Re: Tandon Disk Drive - Serial # 3343
       Invoice # 98115
       Billed to Visa Credit Card #: 4332-1234-8765

Dear Ms. Jackson:

Reference is made to our telephone conversation of today.

I am rejecting the disk drive your company sent me because it is the wrong type. I specifically ordered a double sided, 40-track drive and your company sent me a single sided, 80-track drive.

Enclosed herewith is the disk drive and cable. Either ship another drive and cable by November 1, 1983, or issue a credit to my Visa Card. I will not accept delivery after December 1st.

If you have any questions or comments, please feel free to contact me.

Yours truly,

Ronald Carter

Also state that the list of defects is not limited to what is on the list because there may be unknown defects. Then confirm your call with a letter clearly stating that the goods are rejected and why. See the form letter on page 111. Merely returning the goods without explanation is not sufficient. Otherwise, the seller may claim he did not know you were rejecting them. Keep all paperwork and put the goods in a safe place.

Buyer's Duties

A buyer has certain duties and rights with regard to goods rightfully rejected. If he prepaid for them, he has a "security interest" in them [UCC §2-711(3)]. He can retain possession of them in order to protect his financial investment. He must take reasonable care in safeguarding the goods and hold them for a reasonable period of time to allow the seller to reclaim them. Under UCC §2-602(2)(b), *he does not have to return the rejected goods to the seller.* He must merely make them available for the seller to pick up and reclaim at the seller's expense.

Exception: If you prepaid the goods by credit card and intend to protest the credit card charge (see Chapter 5, "How to Pay"), immediately return them to the seller even if you pay shipping costs yourself. This way you fulfill the credit card company's requirement that you tried in good faith to return them to the seller.

The classical analysis, as adopted by the UCC and the vast majority of the states, provides that a buyer cannot exercise any rights of ownership over rejected goods. If he uses the goods in his home or business as his own property or for his own convenience, he does so in violation of the seller's rights. Such use may negate the rejection and cause a technical acceptance.

One major exception to the classical approach is when the continued use is unavoidable.

> *Example 7-14:* A buyer replaces her black and white CRT tube with a green phosphorous CRT. The tube is defective with lines streaking across it. She may continue to use the computer while waiting for a new CRT tube to be installed or to have her old tube reinstalled.

The classical approach is bending under the realities of everyday life. As one court expressed it:

> We [i.e., the court] do not believe that it would serve the ends of justice to penalize a consumer who exercises his right to reject by prohibiting that consumer from even the slightest use of the goods involved until the conclusion of the litigation. [*Yates vs. Clifford Motors, Inc.,* vs. *Chrysler Corp.,* Pa. Super. 1980, 423 A.2d 1262.]

The theory behind this ruling is that certain goods have become *necessities* in our lives. We become so intertwined with them that we cannot survive in the modern world without them. In *Yates*, the plaintiff continued to *sparingly* use a truck after he had rejected it. The court noted that he had traded in his only car for the truck in question and had no other means of transportation.

In today's society, a microcomputer has not yet reached the point of a *necessity* for most home users. This conclusion is based on the fact that there is nothing for which a home user is using a microcomputer that cannot reasonably be done by other means. It is a rare case with unique facts that would go otherwise.

> *Example 7-15:* You are deaf. Your microcomputer is your major means to communicate with the outside world. You trade in your old microcomputer for a newer model. The newer model has numerous defects, and you properly reject it and demand your old microcomputer back. You can continue to use the newer unit because without it you would have no means of communication.

The classical analysis may also not necessarily be true for the business person who must use the computer for her livelihood. In such a case some use may be allowed.

> *Example 7-16:* A businessperson has a microcomputer in her office. She uses it for word processing, accounting, and so on. She trades it in for a bigger, more powerful unit. After three days of operation, she discovers a major design defect (e.g., the computer cannot add numbers properly), and she notifies the seller that she is rejecting the new computer and demands her old unit back. The seller laughs in her face and says, "Sue me." It is arguable that she could continue to *sparingly* use the new unit for essential purposes such as word processing. The argument is that she has no other way to get the work done.

Seller's Cure

Under UCC §2-508 a seller is allowed to cure his wrongful tender under two circumstances. The first occurs when the time for performance has not yet passed.

> *Example 7-17:* The contract requires delivery of BASF diskettes by June 1st. On May 15, the seller delivers Dysan diskettes. The buyer immediately notifies the seller that the wrong brand was tendered. If the seller says that he will deliver the BASF diskettes prior to June 1, then the buyer will still be obligated to accept the BASF delivery.

The second occurs when the seller could reasonably expect the buyer to accept the wrong tender.

> *Example 7-18:* A buyer orders an Osborne portable computer. At the time of the order Osborne came with only single-density disk drives. The seller takes delivery of the unit from Osborne, which has been "improved" by having double-density disk drives.

If you reject the "improved" model on the grounds that is a wrongful tender, the seller may send you the older model.

Revocation

A buyer's right to revoke a prior acceptance of goods is his greatest protection in the purchase of microcomputer hardware or software. UCC §2-608 allows a buyer who has already accepted goods to revoke the acceptance of a commercial unit whose nonconformity *substantially* impairs its value to him if one of two conditions are met.

Condition 1

The goods were accepted on the assumption that the defect would be fixed, but it has not been fixed within a reasonable period of time.

> *Example 7-19:* A law firm needs a word processing unit that can place footnotes at the bottom of each page. After reviewing advertising claims and speaking with salesmen, the firm buys a system that has this ability. The unit is delivered without the capability. After numerous telephone calls and letters to the seller over a nine-month period, the law firm is advised that the footnoting ability will not be supplied for another 18 months. The firm can revoke its prior acceptance of the computer.

Condition 1 can be particularly important to the buyer of a "lemon computer" when numerous, trivial defects cumulatively add up to a substantial impairment (*Cf. Oberg* vs. *Phillips*, OK App. 1980, 615 P2d 1022, and *Murray* vs. *Holiday Rambler*, 1978, 83 Wis.2d 406, 265 NW2d 513 (1978).

Condition 2

A buyer accepted goods without knowledge of a defect, but the failure to discover the defect was caused by the difficulty of discovering the defect.

> *Example 7-20:* A buyer does a reasonable inspection of an accounting package. Six months later it is discovered that the program rejects any

numerical entry if the fourth digit is a 3 and the second digit is a 5. The seller is notified and acknowledges the bug, but he refuses to fix or repair it.

Warning: As with rejection, once there is a substantial change in the condition of the goods that was not caused by its own defects, acceptance may not be revoked.

> *Example 7-21:* A printer without a friction feed is modified by adding a friction feed.

Time of Revocation

As with rejection, a buyer is obligated to notify the seller of his or her revocation as soon as reasonably possible after discovery of the grounds for revocation.

Warning: Do not attempt to revoke acceptance of any expensive item without getting advice from an attorney or consumer group. Each jurisdiction has different requirements, and failure to fulfill those conditions could void an attempted revocation.

Buyer's Duties

As in rejections, a buyer should not exercise any rights of ownership over the goods other than to hold them safely for return to the seller. If the goods are subsequently used, this could negate any rightful revocation. The exception to this rule has already been discussed—see Examples 7–14 and 7–15.

Practical Considerations

It is best if a buyer never has to revoke or reject an acceptance. Most problems can be avoided if the goods are tested as soon as they arrive. Never let the goods sit several weeks before testing.

Even though the UCC says the buyer does not have to return goods to the seller, he should do so even if it means money out of his pocket. It puts the seller in a worse position   vis-à-vis public relations with the courts, consumer agencies, and other interested parties if the buyer can truthfully claim that the seller has both the buyer's money *and* the goods.

How to Complain Effectively

Effective complaining gets results. Take a case that was reported in the *Manhattan Micro News*, a user group newsletter. A member of the group had a problem with his IBM PC motherboard. Twenty-two days after the 90-day warranty expired, it failed and a repair technician believed the cause was a single, soldered-in RAM chip. IBM's suggestion was to replace the entire motherboard for $1000. Its company's policy did not allow technicians to remove the soldered-in chips. The owner did not get satisfaction until he told IBM and the seller that he would pursue the matter through the Massachusetts court system.

This owner did nothing special. He merely complained effectively. There is no secret to effective complaining. It is necessary only to follow certain tried and true steps. This chapter tells you what steps to follow for working within and outside "the system."

Make Sure You Have a Valid Complaint

Consumers have problems with hardware and software for four main reasons.

The first reason is the fundamental difference between microcomputer hardware and software and other consumer goods—their complexity. You cannot turn them on like a television set and expect them to work.

Example 8-1: To operate some word processing systems fully, more than 70 different key strokes must be learned.

Second, there is no uniformity in the microcomputer industry. Once you know how to drive a car, you can drive any automobile. Change your computer and software, and you must start over at square one.

Third, most documentation lacks detail and is poorly written.

Example 8-2: One major word processing program has the ability to generate mandatory spaces. It is possible to make sure that city names such as "St. Louis" or "New York" are not printed on two separate lines. Nowhere in the documentation are there instructions on how to use this capability.

Fourth, many people refuse to read instruction manuals. It is easier for them to call the local store expert than to open the manual.

How to Communicate the Problem

A hardware or software problem is not a bona fide problem until it happens more than once to more than one person. If it happens only once to one individual, it could be caused by numerous items, such as fluctuating electricity or operator error, that are not related to the hardware or software. If the problem begins to occur elsewhere, the cause probably is limited to the hardware or software.

Hardware Problems

Whenever hardware problems arise, make a record of the symptoms so that you can repeatedly describe them in the same manner. Know under what particular circumstances they show up. Ascertain if the problem is continuous or intermittent. Be able to demonstrate your problem when taking the unit in for repair.

Software Problems

Software problems, especially random bugs, are the most difficult problems to solve. Theoretically, every program has undergone extensive testing before being released and has been thoroughly "debugged." Therefore, your "bug" should not have occurred. Add to this the problem of operator error. Many times what seems to be a "bug" is actually how the program works. Had you read the instruction manual in greater detail, this would have been apparent.

Saying that a problem exists is not sufficient. As with a hardware problem, being able to consistently generate the problem or giving the author or vendor a diskette to examine that clearly shows the "bug" is to win half the battle.

> *Example 8-3:* Personal Software's CCA Data Management System published a series of "Fixnotes" that cured the problems users were having, such as getting the addition totals rounded off (e.g., $12,435.72 became $12,436.00).

Hint: When having hardware or software repaired, write a detailed letter explaining the problem. Make sure to include documentary evidence such as an unreadable diskette or illegible printouts when taking the unit in (make copies for your records). If you ship your goods to a repair center, make another copy and mail it separately.

Problems with New Peripherals

Just because the vendor says a hardware or software package is compatible does not mean it actually is! A recurrent problem with microcomputers is that the hardware or software fails when a new peripheral or patch is added. Most times, even though the problem seems unrelated to the new addition, the new peripheral or patch has caused the problem.

If the hardware or software was working fine until the new peripheral or patch was added, disconnect the new equipment or reverse the patch and see what happens. If the problem goes away, the new patch or peripheral has undoubtedly created the problem.

Keeping Good Records

Store all sales slips, credit card vouchers, cancelled checks, repair tickets, advertisements, and the like that deal with your microcomputer purchases in a separate place, such as in a file folder.

Good records are very important when there is a recurring problem that no one has been able to fix. Confronting a dealer or manufacturer with the previous repair tickets will negate the claim that there has not been a sufficient opportunity to effectuate a repair. The repair tickets will be the proof that the manufacturer's warranty has failed in its essential purpose.

Note the day the equipment was taken in and returned. Make sure your copy of the repair ticket is readable. Customers typically get the unreadable second or third carbon copy.

When you call about a problem, get the name (have it spelled) of the person you are speaking with. As soon as the conversation ends, write down the name, the date, the time of the call, and what was said by whom. This way you have a contemporaneous writing that can later be used to refresh your memory.

Repair Services

Always get a receipt when leaving equipment with anybody for any purpose. Otherwise, there may be no record of your leaving the equipment.

Repair receipts typically state that the repair center is "Not Liable For Goods Left Over 30 Days" or "Not Liable For Loss of Equipment." These words have no legal effect. If the repair center loses your equipment, it is liable for its current value (usually less than replacement cost). Also, a repair service cannot sell your equipment if you do not immediately pick it up. Most states have statutes on this point that say the goods have to be held a certain length of time before they can be disposed of. Contact a local consumer group for your state's specific requirements.

Not all "factory authorized repair centers" will fix your computer under the warranty terms. Some repair only equipment that they sold. Also, find out how the warranty bill will be paid. Some repair centers require you to pay personally for the repair work; you then file a claim for reimbursement against the manufacturer or warrantor. A repair center can retain possession of your equipment until you (or the warrantor) pay for the work.

Unless you have prior experience with a particular repair service, do not assume that the equipment has actually been fixed. Test it before paying for it or taking it home.

> *Example 8-4:* A client bought a defective television set from a national retail chain. The sound would fade away and disappear. Over 18 months, it was "repaired" three times. After the third repair, the client asked the service manager to prove that the set had been repaired. The service manager turned it on and three minutes later the sound disappeared. The client then got a new television set.

If the equipment does not work perfectly when you pick it up, write that fact on the receipt you are asked to sign. Get the service technician to initial your comment. If he will not, write the fact that he refused on the ticket.

Dealing with Your Problem within the System

Always give the seller the first chance to repair the equipment. He has a vested interest in keeping his customers happy and retaining their good will. Other authorized dealers, although they may repair the unit under the warranty terms, may not give as quick or good service to you as they would to their own customers. This unfortunate result arises because warranty repairs are typically reimbursed for a lower rate than would be charged if the customer paid the bill directly.

Know What You Want

Before complaining, decide on the minimum you will accept. Do you want your money back? Do you want the unit replaced? Do you want it fixed? Decide before making your complaint, and stick with that demand. It is a good tactic to ask for more than you think you can get. This way, if you do not get your original demand, you appear magnanimous when settling for less.

Confirm the Settlement Terms in Writing

When settling any complaints, get the terms in writing. If the other party refuses to write you, then write him or her a letter stating what your understanding of the settlement is. If you fail to do this, nothing prevents the other party from claiming, "I never said that," or "You misunderstood what I meant." If you write a letter expressing your understanding of a settlement and the other party does not object to its contents, he looks bad when he later says you are wrong.

Be Prompt

If you are instructed to bring or ship the unit back for repairs or replacement, do it *now*—not next week. The sooner it is done, the better. Have you received a letter in response to a complaint? Answer it immediately, and follow its instructions. If you are lackadaisical, so will the other party be.

Work Your Way Up the Ladder

In dealing with a problem, find out who in the company can resolve it, and start dealing with him or her. This person is generally a department, store, or service manager. If someone says he cannot resolve your complaint or he does not have the authority to do what you want, ask

FIGURE 8-1

RONALD CARTER
1404 E. Central
Jackson, MO 63001

February 1, 1984

Corporation Division
Secretary of State's Office
500 S. Main Street
Sacramento, CA 95651

Re: The Disk Shop
      1901 Byte Drive
      Los Angeles, CA 91711

Dear Sir:

      I would like to know the names and addresses of the
corporate officers of the above name company. If it is not a
corporation could you please check under the registered
fictitious names.

      If there is a charge for this service, please let me know.

      I look forward to hearing from you. If you have any
questions, please feel free to contact me.

                    Yours truly,

                    Ronald Carter

FIGURE 8-2

RONALD CARTER
1404 E. Central
Jackson, MO 63001

March 15, 1983

Ms. Johanna Green
President
Microcomputer Shoppes, Ltd.
34232 7th Avenue
Los Angeles, CA 97222

Re: GeeWhiz Computer - Model # 1023
      Serial # 92-3131
      Your repairs tickets: ##3451, 4532, and 5532

Dear Ms. Green:

On December 15, 1982, I purchased the above computer from your St. Louis store. It was to be used to keep my business books and provide word processing. To date, it has spent more times in repairs than in my possession.

It has been returned three times for the same repairs; the disk drives go crazy and destroy any information contained on the diskettes. Twice I demonstrated this problem to your local service technician and he attempted to fix it. On the third time, I requested that he ship the unit back to GeeWhiz for repairs. Allegedly it was; yet when the unit was returned to me on February 28, 1983, it did not work.

At that point, I showed the computer to your local manager, Mr. Henry. He attempted to operate the computer and failed. He then wanted to try a fourth time to fix it. I told him that was unacceptable and requested that he either (1) refund my money or (2) replace the unit. He refused stating company policy stated all he could do was repair it. For that reason I am appealing to you.

I have been more than reasonable in allowing your corporation and GeeWhiz an attempt to repair the computer. It is obvious to me this computer is a lemon. No matter how many times this particular computer is "repaired" I will not be satisfied with it. I feel I can trust neither you nor GeeWhiz to return a trouble free computer to me. I have been so aggravated by he situation, that I would rather write the computer off than have it allegedly "repaired" again.

FIGURE 8-2 *(cont.)*

letter to Johanna Green
page 2

    I bought a GeeWhiz computer because of its reputation for high quality. I bought the computer at Microcomputer Shoppe because of your reputation for fairness and customer satisfaction. Know that I am an unsatisfied customer who is both disappointed in the quality of the computer and the quality of the repair service done on it.

    I would like you to either authorize a refund of my purchase price or an exchange of my present computer for another GeeWhiz computer.

    I look forward to hearing from you.

                Yours truly,

                Ronald Carter

him for the name and address of the person who has the authority. Write a letter to that person, and refer to your dealings with the first person. If the first person will not give you the name of his superior, write to the president of the company. The name and address of the president can usually be found by writing to the Secretary of State's Office, Corporation Division, in any state in which the company is licensed to do business. The state mentioned in the company's advertising literature is usually where its corporate headquarters are located. For a nominal fee, the Secretary of State of that state will send you a form with the information you need. See the letter on page 121.

Do not be afraid to go to the top. One of the nicer aspects of dealing with a large corporation is that you can always work your way up the hierarchy of the corporate officers. The only person who can ultimately say "No" is the president. On page 122 is an example of a letter to a company president.

The letter should be brief and to the point. If there are many problems, ignore the minor ones. Do not become apologetic, yet do not appear to be domineering. You want to appear to be an everyday consumer who has a legitimate complaint against the company.

This letter will go to the owner or president. Usually, you will get a call or letter saying to bring the equipment in. If there is more than one service technician, the best one will be assigned to repair your equipment. He will now work his butt off trying to fix the equipment because he knows his boss is concerned with your happiness. He knows you will not hesitate to write a second letter saying you brought it in but that it was still not fixed.

Applying Pressure to Get Results

The reason for applying pressure is to get more people involved in your problem who have an interest in it and the product involved.

Before you can apply pressure, you must take care of the following points:

1. Write a clear and concise statement of the facts, using as much detail as possible.
2. Prepare full documentation. Make clear photocopies of all repair tickets, sale slips, letters, and the like.
3. Decide exactly what redress you want.

Step 1: Write to the Manufacturer

Write to the president of the company that manufactures the goods involved. If a local store or mail order company does not care if you

FIGURE 8-3

RONALD CARTER
1404 E. Central
Jackson, MO 63001

April 1, 1983

Mr. Ren Dubois, President
GeeWhiz Computer Company
314 East Fifth Avenue
New York, NY 16021

Re: GeeWhiz Computer
     Serial # 92-3131

Dear Mr. Dubois:

On December 15, 1982, I purchased the above computer from Microcomputer Shoppes in St. Louis. The computer has been nothing but trouble. Twice, Microcomputer Shoppes technicians tried to fix it. It was even returned to the "factory" for repair. Still it does not work. On February 28, 1983, I requested that Microcomputer Shoppes either replace it or refund my money. This request was denied by the store manager, Mr. Henry. He informed me all he could do was "repair" the computer.

I have been more than reasonable in giving your authorized sales representatives and your corporation three attempts to fix my computer. I have lived up to the terms of your warranty by returning it for repairs. Your company has failed these terms by not fixing the computer.

Since neither you nor Microcomputer Shoppes have been able to fix the computer, I feel you should replace it or refund my money.

I have been more than reasonable in this situation. It is obvious to me this computer is a lemon. No matter how many times this particular computer is "repaired" I will not be satisfied with it. I have been so aggravated by the situation, that I would rather write the computer off than have it allegedly "repaired" again.

I would like you to either authorize Microcomputer Shoppes to exchange my computer or make the exchange yourself.

I look forward to hearing from you.

Yours truly,

Ronald Carter

have problems, the manufacturer will. Write a letter describing your travails with the local store, and ask for help in resolving the problem. If the local store is a franchise, write the franchisor and complain. A sample letter to a company president is shown in Figure 8-3 on page 125.

Step 2: Write a Few Well-Placed Letters

If you do not get satisfaction from the manufacturer, it is time to increase the pressure and try to compel the manufacturer to make you happy.

The easiest way to apply pressure is to write a few well-placed letters. Letters can be written to magazines in which the company advertises, local consumer groups, government officials, and the like. *Every time you send a letter to someone, send a copy to the company.*

Write to Magazines.   Write to any and all computer magazines you read in which the company advertises. You do not have to be a subscriber. A typical letter might resemble the one in Figure 8-4.

Do not expect major action out of the magazine. All it will do is write the company a letter and ask the company to check it out and respond to the magazine. Usually the magazine will send you a letter stating it can be only a conduit for discussion and asking you to inform it if and when the problem is resolved. What is not clearly stated is the magazine's power. If it gets enough complaints about a company, it will alert its readers.

> *Example 8-5:* In the April, 1983, issue of 80-Micro, the editors issued the following 80 Alert:
>
> "We've received five letters concerning Shannon Magnetics or Data Resources. . . . In each case, the reader ordered supplies, mostly disks, and paid by credit card. Although the credit cards were charged immediately, the supplies never arrived.
>
> Shannon Magnetics told customers that the disks were back-ordered. The company agreed to send refunds, but customers report they never received them.
>
> We [80-Micro] have not been able to contact Shannon Magnetics. The company's telephone numbers have been disconnected, and they have not answered correspondence. So far, we have been unable to obtain any further information."

Send the same letter to each magazine the company advertises in.

Write to Government Officials.   Write to the President of the United States at the White House, Washington, D.C. 20500.

FIGURE 8-4

RONALD CARTER
1404 E. Central
Jackson, MO 63001

April 30, 1983

Ms. Karen Makwoz
Advertising Compliance
Prestigious Computer Magazine
1340 East Michigan Avenue
New York, NY 10012

Re: The Software Shoppe
       29 McPherson Avenue
       Phoenix, Arizona

Dear Ms. Makwoz:

I would like your help in resolving a problem I am having with the above mentioned advertisers. Its most recent advertisement appeared on page 85 of your April, 1983 issue.

On January 15, 1983, I ordered Benson's Data Base Management program.   I sent them my personal check for $140. The check cleared January 28th. To date I have not received the program. I have written three letters but I have not gotten a response.

One of the reasons I ordered this product was that it was advertised in your magazine. Your magazine has always had the highest reputation and I am sure you are not happy that your advertisers are behaving in this manner.

Copies of the check and letters are enclosed. I would deeply appreciate any help you can give me in resolving this problem.

I look forward to hearing from you. If you have any questions, please feel free to contact me.

                    Yours truly,

                    Ronald Carter

The president's staff includes the Office of Consumer Affairs. This office advises the president on consumer affairs. Your letter will be forwarded to the appropriate government agency.

Also write your congressman and senators. Ask them to forward your complaint to the appropriate Congressional committee that deals with your problem.

Write the Federal Trade Commission.   Write to the Federal Trade Commission's Bureau of Consumer Protection, Washington, D.C. 20580.

The Federal Trade Commission rarely acts on individual complaints, but if it gets enough complaints from different individuals, it will investigate.

Write to the Attorney General.   Write to the attorney generals of the state where the company is incorporated or doing business and your state. A sample letter appears on page 129.

Supply them with details of your complaints, proof of payment, attempts to resolve the problem, and so on. Tell them that you are unhappy with the company and feel that it may be guilty of consumer fraud. Ask them to investigate. If the company is local, complain to your local district attorney, especially if you feel that you were the victim of a fraud or some deceptive practices. If the facts are bad enough, the prosecutor may file criminal charges. Although you may not recover your loss, your letter may help prevent someone else from suffering a loss.

Contact the Consumer Hot Line

If a local newspaper or television station has an "Action Line" or "Hotline" type of reporting, give it the facts. If your case can be presented as a good guy versus bad guy, if the facts can be briefly and simply explained, and if the case appears to be loaded with injustice, a reporter may investigate. Nothing scares any business more (whether honest or not) than learning that a local newspaper or television station is pursuing a story dealing with alleged bad consumer practices on the part of that business.

Contact the Postal Inspector

If you feel you have been defrauded and the U.S. mail was involved, complain to the local postal inspector's office. Your local post office can tell you how to contact the nearest inspector's office.

FIGURE 8-5

RONALD CARTER
1404 E. Central
Jackson, MO 63001

April 1, 1983

Department of Consumer Affairs
Attorney General's Office
State of New York
Albany, NY 12333

Re: GeeWhiz Computer Company
     New York, NY

Dear Sirs:

I would like your help in resolving a dispute I am having with GeeWhiz Computer Company.

Last November, I purchased a GeeWhiz Computer, Serial # 92-3131. The computer has never worked properly. Twice its authorized repair service in St. Louis, attempted to fix it. Last February, it was returned to the "factory" for repair. It came back inoperable. I have written both the vendor and GeeWhiz numerous letters expressing my displeasure that the unit still fails to work. Photocopies of all correspondence and repair tickets are enclosed.

GeeWhiz has never responded to my inquiries. I do not think it is right that GeeWhiz has my money and I have a defective computer that it either cannot or will not repair.

I would appreciate it if you could investigate this matter or give me any suggestions as how I might proceed.

I look forward to hearing from you.

Yours truly,

Ronald Carter

Various Tricks of the Trade

Certified Mail.   A favorite delaying ploy used by manufacturers and suppliers is to say "This is the first I have heard of it," or "I do not have any record of receiving your complaint." Get around this ploy by sending your complaint letters certified mail, return receipt requested. The post office charges approximately $1.55 for this service. Before the letter will be given to the recipient, he must sign an official receipt, which is then returned to you. The receipt is proof that your letter was delivered.

Type your Letters.   Many people have trouble communicating their problems. The situation is worsened when the company or vendor cannot read a complaint letter. Type the letter if possible. If you do not have or cannot get access to a typewriter, make sure your letter is legible and easily understood. Before mailing it, get someone else to read it because you are too close to the problem to be objective. This person will catch your spelling mistakes and tell you if the letter makes sense.

Documentation.   *Always document a complaint.* Send photocopies of invoices, repair tickets, and the like. Do not send the original documents. Most public libraries and post offices have copy machines available for public use.

Fighting Dirty

After everything we have previously discussed has failed, it is time to bring out the heavy artillery. Do not take lightly the tactics described in the following paragraphs. They are the equivalent of declaring war.

Getting Legal Help

Most times, hiring a lawyer to resolve a consumer dispute is only throwing good money after bad. Lawyers cost money. With hourly rates ranging from $45 per hour on up, the legal bill can quickly overshadow the amount of money involved.

This is not to say that lawyers do not have their place. Sometimes a letter from a lawyer can work wonders. If you feel a lawyer must be hired, try to get him to give you a fixed fee for only a letter. Then see what happens. It may not be necessary for the lawyer to do more than this.

When you hire a lawyer, find one who is familiar with consumer and warranty law. A good place to start looking is for a lawyer who has poverty law experience. His or her previous clients will have had more consumer problems than the average person, and it is likely that this lawyer will know consumer law.

If a lawsuit is filed, make sure it is brought under the Magnuson–Moss Warranty Act (see Chapter 6, "Law of Warranties," for a complete discussion) because Magnuson–Moss allows you to recover your attorney's fees if you win.

Magazine and Newspaper Advertising

The United States Constitution guarantees free speech, but the realities of business being what they are, very few computer magazines and newspapers will bite the hands that feed them. If your complaint is against a large advertiser, you could be 100% in the right, but the magazine is not likely to run a critical article in fear of losing the advertising.

Computer magazines and newspapers are not without purpose. You can exercise your freedom of speech by running a truthful advertisement in them yourself. Most magazines have a section in which consumers can advertise their spare equipment and software. Think of the reaction if you were to run the following advertisement:

> My Acme microcomputer is a lemon. Is yours? If so, add your name to a list of dissatisfied customers. Send your name, address, and your major complaint to Ronald Carter, 1040 E. Central, Jackson, MO 63001.

If you can give a magazine, the Federal Trade Commission, or any other consumer agency proof that there are many dissatisfied customers who have the same complaint, they will take notice. No longer is it just you; it is a large group (see Example 8-5).

Alternatively, offer your microcomputer for sale. Consider the effect of the following advertisement:

> *For Sale:* GeeWhiz Model 100 Microcomputer with 2 GeeWhiz disk drives, extended memory, and much more. New cost $2000; will sacrifice for $1500 or best offer for following reasons: keyboard freezes up twice a day; disk drive crashes and loses data once a week; intermittent memory problems; interference with all televisions and radios within 100 feet, and much more. If interested, call Ronald Carter (314-123-4567), or write 1404 E. Central, Jackson, MO 63001.

So long as the advertisement is truthful, it is protected by the First Amendment. However, be warned that if you use a false statement, you can be sued for libel.

If there is a local computer festival, rent a booth to sell your machine. Make a sign similar to the "For Sale" advertisement.

Give the Unit Away

If you can afford to give the unit away, make a gift of it to the president of the manufacturing company. Write him or her a detailed letter stating what is wrong with the unit and saying that you are making a gift of it to him or her. Ship the unit off, and send copies of your letter to the various computer magazines. Because this is equivalent to a "man bites dog" story, some magazines may publish it. Alternatively, give the unit to a charity, and take a charitable deduction off your income taxes.

Miscellaneous Hints and Suggestions

Telephone Calls

Never pay for a long distance telephone call unless you have to. Before calling long distance, contact WATS information, 800-555-1212, and ask if the company you wish to call has a WATS line. If no WATS number is listed, call collect. When the operator asks your name, say that you are a customer and want to ask a question or place an order. Instruct the operator to repeat that to the person who answers the phone. In most cases, the company will accept the charges. If the call is not accepted, hang up and direct dial. Do not offer to pay for the call because you will be billed at the higher operator-assisted rate. As soon as the telephone is answered, ask the person if the company has a WATS line you can call in on (some companies have unlisted WATS lines). If the answer is "Yes," get the number and call back on it.

Some companies list two numbers in their advertisements. One is a WATS number and for "orders only"; the other is not a WATS line and is for any other purpose. Always use the WATS number regardless of what you want. At worst, you will be told to call back on the other line.

Shipments

When you ship a package across the country or across town, use United Parcel Service or another delivery service. The cost is normally equivalent to or cheaper than the post office charge. Delivery is quicker, and the recipient has to sign a receipt for the package. If you use the post office, send the package by certified mail, return receipt requested, and if necessary, insure the contents. Do not drop the package in a mail box. Take it inside the post office, and get an official stamp on the certified mail receipt.

Duplicating the Manual

With all non-game software, get a duplicate instruction manual; either buy it from the manufacturer or photocopy the one that came with the software. Put the duplicate in a safe, secure area. This duplication is necessary because many software companies will not sell manuals to individuals in an effort to suppress piracy. Think of the position you would be in if the original manual were destroyed or lost, and you had forgotten how to access certain data. Duplication is a cheap form of insurance.

Mailing Containers

Save all mailing containers! When a package arrives, do not rip it open. Carefully open it so as not to destroy the packaging. Then, if the item must be returned, you have a proper shipping container. An added bonus is that a vendor has a difficult time arguing that the goods were damaged in shipment back to him, because you used the same container he used.

Where to Put the Computer

Many microcomputer advertisements show the unit on the back of a truck, in a kitchen, or on the floor. These advertisements demonstrate only the advertising agency's lack of actual microcomputer experience.

A microcomputer is a delicate piece of machinery. It does not like being jostled about. Dust, whether it be dirt or flour, can destroy diskettes and damage disk drives. Treat the computer gently, and it will last forever. Treat it roughly, and it will bankrupt you with repair bills.

Hardware Modifications

Do not buy a hardware modification based only on an advertisement. Examine the installation and operations manuals. Most manufacturers sell these manuals as separate items and give credit for their purchase price when the hardware is bought. Many times the manuals will state important limitations that are not mentioned in the advertisement.

The operations manual, beside telling how to operate the modification, should describe in detail what the modification can and cannot do. A determination can then be made whether the modification will actually fulfill your needs.

Even a brief scan of the installation manual can determine whether you can install the modification. What a manufacturer describes as a "simple 30-minute job that even the most inexperienced owner can complete" may be far beyond your ability.

NEVER personally install a hardware modification unless cost is of primary concern or you have previous electronics experience. The cost of having a trained professional make the installation is minor compared to the cost of the hardware. For a small sum you can be assured (1) that the modification works as expected and (2) that it was installed properly. Furthermore, the professional can more easily determine whether bad parts were delivered and make any necessary fine adjustments.

> Example 9-1: A St. Louis Radio Shack Computer Center charges $45 to install the two internal disk drives ($1000) in a TRS-80 Model III. The local Microcomputer Technology Dealer charges $50 to install MTI's $849 CP/Mb upgrade kit.

Hardware improperly installed can do enormous damage to the computer and to you. Just think what would happen if the video monitor or a board of RAM chips were improperly grounded.

Sound

Most microcomputers can generate a wide variety of sounds if an audio output device is attached or built in. The most common use of these devices is to generate the "pop" and "boom" on video arcade games. Do not expect a microcomputer to reproduce subtle sounds. Even if it could, a microcomputer could not teach you to speak a foreign language because it could neither hear nor correct your mispronunciation.

If an audio output device is an extra cost option, do not buy it on a business or personal computer. If it will be used for educational purposes, such as teaching a child how to spell, it may be a worthwhile investment.

Service Contracts

A service contract is an agreement whereby someone, for a fixed annual fee, agrees to maintain, repair, and replace broken or worn parts if your microcomputer needs it. The main selling "pitch" behind a service contract is that you are protected from "unexpected" repair bills. Do not fall for this claim. A service contract is not sold as a favor; the company selling it expects to make a profit on it. It expects the income from the service contract to be greater than the sum it will expend maintaining your computer. Service contracts are not cheap. The average yearly cost is between 12 and 20% of the microcomputer's new purchase price.

There are four primary levels of service contracts. Each level is more expensive than the preceding level, as shown in the following list:

1. The equipment must be carried into the shop for service, and it will be repaired in the order it was received.
2. Same as #1, except the equipment will be next in line to be repaired.
3. A service technician will come to where the equipment is located and attempt to repair it there. Calls are responded to in the order they are received.
4. Same as #3, except your call becomes the technician's next call.

The major problem with items 2 and 4 is what happens when the technician has more than one machine or call waiting. Two machines cannot be repaired at the same time.

Before a service contract is bought, ask the following questions:

1. When does the service contract begin? Does it start immediately or only after the manufacturer's original warranty expires?
2. Does the contract have to be bought when the equipment is purchased, or can it be bought later? If later, are there any special conditions such as that the hardware must be brought into the shop for an extra-cost inspection?
3. What is the cost of the service contract in the second, third, and later years? Are these prices fixed, or can they be raised? If they can be raised, are there any limitations? (Get these answers in writing!)
4. Can the entity offering the service contract refuse to renew it, and if so, under what circumstances?
5. Who is offering the service contract? If it is the vendor, is it under the auspices of the manufacturer, or is it totally independent?
6. Does the service contract run with the equipment, or is it personal to you (important if you sell the equipment)?

7. Can a service contract be purchased for only selected equipment, or must the entire system be covered? What can be done if equipment (e.g., a disk drive) is added or deleted?
8. What does the service contract cover? Does it cover all contingencies (e.g., the building gets hit by lightning and 20,000 volts go through the computer), or is it limited? If it is limited, to what circumstances?
9. What do you do if the equipment cannot be fixed quickly (e.g., parts must be ordered from across the country)? Will a loaner be provided?

Should a Service Contract Be Purchased?

To the microcomputer owner who uses the equipment less than full time, a service contract is a bad investment. With present day quality control, a electronic component will either work or not work when it is first powered up. If it works then, it should continue to work for years without trouble. The mechanical pieces, such as the keyboard, disk drives, switches, and the like, are what wear out. They can move only so many times before their useful life is over. To make matters worse, by the time the parts finally need to be replaced, the equipment is no longer made and the parts may be unavailable.

The business user is in a different category. His or her microcomputer is used so often that heavy stress is placed on it. Such a user has a greater chance of the equipment breaking or wearing out than does the nonbusiness user, and should carefully consider buying a contract.

Protect Yourself

No one can protect you against fraud except yourself. If a deal seems too good to be true, it probably is. If everyone else is selling the ACME printer for $400, and some dealer offers to sell one for $200 prepaid, ask yourself "Why?"

Index